D1624096

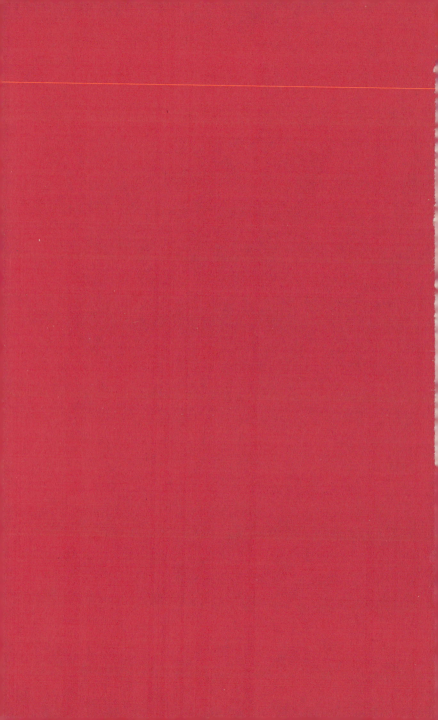

THe MEANiNg Of LIFF

Also by Douglas Adams

The Hitchhiker's Guide to the Galaxy
The Restaurant at the End of the Universe
Life, The Universe and Everything

DOUGLAS ADAMS & JOHN LLOYD

THE MEANING OF LIFF

Harmony Books/New York

With grateful thanks to Jane Belson, Gaye Green, Sean Hardie, Alex Catto, Laurie Rowley, Peter Spence, Helen Rhys Jones, and Caroline Warner for some of the more interesting and repellent ideas in this book.

Copyright © 1984 by Douglas Adams and John Lloyd.
All rights reserved. No part of this book may be reproduced or transmitted in any form or by any means, electronic or mechanical, including photocopying, recording, or by any information storage and retrieval system, without permission in writing from the publisher.

Published by Harmony Books, a division of Crown Publishers, Inc., One Park Avenue, New York, New York 10016.

HARMONY and colophon are trademarks of Crown Publishers, Inc.

Manufactured in the United States of America

Library of Congress Cataloging on Publication Data

Adams, Douglas, 1952–
  The meaning of liff.

  1. American wit and humor. 2. Names, Geographical—United States—Anecdotes, facetiae, satire, etc.
I. Lloyd, John. II. Title.
PN6231.N24A3 1984 910'.207 83-26469
ISBN 0-517-55347-3

10 9 8 7 6 5 4 3 2 1
First American Edition

In Life,* there are many hundreds of common experiences, feelings, situations, and even objects that we all know and recognize, but for which no words exist.

On the other hand, the world is littered with thousands of spare words that spend their time doing nothing but loafing about on signposts pointing at places.

Our job, as we see it, is to get these words down off the signpost and into the mouths of babes and sucklings and so on, where they can start earning their keep in everyday conversation and make a more positive contribution to society.

Douglas Adams
John Lloyd

*And, indeed, in Liff.

Aasleagh (n.) A liqueur made only for drinking at the end of a revoltingly long bottle party when all the drinkable drink has been drunk.

Aberbeeg (vb.) Of amateur actors, to adopt a Mexican accent when called upon to play any variety of foreigner (except Pakistanis—for whom a Welsh accent is considered sufficient).

Abercrave (vb.) To strongly desire to swing from the pole on the rear platform of a bus.

Aberystwyth (n.) A nostalgic yearning that is more pleasant than the thing being yearned for.

Abilene (adj.) Descriptive of the pleasing coolness of the reverse side of the pillow.

Abinger (n.) One who washes everything except the frying pan, the cheese grater, and the saucepan that the chocolate sauce was made in.

Aboyne (vb.) To beat an expert at a game of skill by playing so appallingly that none of his clever tactics or strategies are of any use to him.

Acle (n.) The rogue pin that shirtmakers conceal in the most improbable fold of a new shirt. Its function is to stab you when you don the garment.

Adlestrop (n.) That part of a suitcase which is designed to get snarled up on conveyor belts at airports. Some of the more modern adlestrop designs have a special quick-release feature that enables the case to flip open at this point and fling your underwear into the conveyor belt's gearing mechanism.

Adrigole (n.) The centerpiece of a merry-go-round on which the man with the tickets stands unnervingly still.

Affcot (n.) The sort of fart you hope people will talk after.

Affpuddle (n.) A puddle that is hidden under a pivoted paving stone. You know it's there only when you step on the paving stone and the puddle shoots up your leg.

Ahenny (adj.) The way people stand when examining other people's bookshelves.

Aigburth (n.) Any piece of readily identifiable anatomy found in cooked meat.

Ainderby Quernhow (n.) One who continually be-moans the loss of the word *gay* to the English language, even though they had never used the word in any context at all until they started complaining that they couldn't use it anymore.

Ainderby Steeple (n.) One who asks you a question with the apparent motive of wanting to hear your answer, but cuts short your opening sentence by leaning forward and saying, "And I'll tell you why I ask..." and then talking solidly for the next hour.

Ainsworth (n.) The length of time it takes to get served in a camera shop. Hence, also, how long we will have to wait for the abolition of income tax or the Second Coming.

Aird of Sleat (n. archaic) Ancient Scottish curse placed from afar on the stretch of land now occupied by Heathrow Airport.

Aith (n.) The single bristle that sticks out sideways on a cheap paintbrush.

Albuquerque (n.) A shapeless squiggle that is utterly unlike your normal signature, but that is, nevertheless, all you are able to produce when asked formally to identify yourself. Muslims, whose religion forbids the making of graven images, use albuquerques to decorate their towels, menu cards, and pajamas.

Aldclune (n.) One who collects ten-year-old telephone directories.

Alltami (n.) The ancient art of being able to balance the hot and cold shower taps.

Ambleside (n.) A talk given about the facts of life by a father to his son while walking in the garden on a Sunday afternoon.

Amersham (n.) The sneeze that tickles but never comes. (Thought to derive from the London subway station of the same name, where the rails always rattle but the train never arrives.)

Amlwch (n.) A vending-machine sandwich that has been kept soft by being regularly washed and resealed in plastic wrap.

Araglin (n. archaic) A medieval practical joke played by young squires on a knight aspirant the afternoon he is due to start his vigil. When the knight arrives at the castle, the squires raise the drawbridge very suddenly as the knight and his charger step onto it.

Ardcrony (n.) A remote acquaintance passed off as "a very good friend of mine" by someone trying to impress people.

Ardscalpsie (n.) Excuse made by rural Welsh hairdresser for completely massacring your hair.

Ardscull (n.) Excuse made by rural Welsh hairdresser for deep wounds inflicted on your scalp in an attempt to rectify whatever it was that induced the ardscalpsie (q.v.)

Ardslignish (adj.) Adjective that describes the behavior of Scotch tape when you are tired.

Articlave (n.) A clever architectural construction designed to give the illusion from the top deck of a bus that it is far too big for the road.

Aynho (vb.) Of waiters, never to have a pen.

B

Babworth (n.) Something that justifies having a really good cry.

Baldock (n.) The sharp prong on the top of a tree stump where the tree snapped off before being completely sawed through.

Ballycumber (n.) One of the six half-read books lying somewhere in your bed.

Banff (adj.) Pertaining to, or descriptive of, that kind of facial expression which is impossible to achieve except when having a passport photograph taken.

Banteer (n. archaic) A lusty and raucous old ballad sung after a particularly spectacular araglin (q.v.) has been pulled off.

Baraboo (n.) The final scene in a situation comedy when the plot has been resolved and the whole cast reassembles for one last very tiny joke before the credits and the hemorrhoid commercials.

Barstibley (n.) A humorous device such as a china horse or small naked porcelain infant that jocular hosts use to piss water into your Scotch with.

Baughurst (n.) That kind of large fierce ugly woman who owns a small fierce ugly dog.

Baumber (n.) A fitted elasticized bottom sheet that turns your mattress banana-shaped.

Bealings (pl. n. archaic) The unsavory parts of a moat that a knight has to pour out of his armor after being the victim of an araglin (q.v.). In medieval Flanders, soup made from bealings was a very slightly sought-after delicacy.

Beaulieu hill (n.) The optimum vantage point from which to view people undressing in the bedroom across the street.

Beccles (pl.n.) The small bone buttons placed in bacon sandwiches by unemployed guerrilla dentists.

Bedfont (n.) A lurching sensation in the pit of the stomach experienced at breakfast in a hotel, occasioned by the realization that it is about now that the chambermaid will have discovered the embarrassing stain on your bottom sheet.

Belper (n.) A wad of someone else's chewing gum that you unexpectedly find your hand resting on under a desk top, under the passenger seat of your car, or on somebody's thigh under her skirt.

Benburb (n.) The sort of man who becomes a returning officer.

Berepper (n.) The irrevocable and sturdy fart released in the presence of royalty, which sounds quite like a small motorbike passing by (but not enough to be confused with one).

Berkhamsted (n.) The massive three-course midmorning pig-out enjoyed by a dieter who has already done his or her dieting duty by having a teaspoonful of cottage cheese for breakfast.

Berry Pomeroy (n.) l. The shape of a gourmet's lips. 2. The droplet of saliva that hangs from them.

Bilbster (n.) A pimple so hideous and enormous that you have to cover it with an adhesive bandage and pretend you cut yourself shaving.

Bishop's Caundle (n.) An opening gambit before a game of chess whereby the missing pieces are replaced by small ornaments from the mantelpiece.

Blean (n.) Scientific measure of luminosity: 1 glimmer = 100,000 bleans. Usherettes' flashlights are designed to produce between 2.5 and 4 bleans, enabling them to assist you in falling downstairs or treading on people.

Blithbury (n.) A look someone gives you by which you become aware that they're much too drunk to have understood anything you've said to them in the last twenty minutes.

Blitterlees (pl. n.) The little slivers of bamboo picked off a cane chair by a nervous guest, which litter the carpet beneath and tell the chair's owner that the whole piece of furniture is about to uncoil terribly and slowly until it resembles a giant pencil sharpening.

Blount (n.) One who knows absolutely nothing whatsoever about the Russian people except for the fact that he hates them.

Bodmin (n.) The irrational and inevitable discrepancy between the amount pooled and the amount needed when a large group of people try to pay a bill together after a meal.

Bolsover (n.) One of those brown plastic trays with bumps, placed upside down in boxes of chocolates to make you think you're getting two layers.

Bonkle (n.) Of plumbing in old hotels, to make loud and unexplained noises in the night, particularly at about five o'clock in the morning.

Boolteens (pl. n.) The small scatterings of foreign coins that inhabit dressing tables. Since they are never used, boolteens account for a significant drain on the world's money supply.

Boothby Graffoe (n.) 1. The man in the bar who slaps people on the back as if they were old friends, when in fact he has no friends, largely on account of this habit. 2. Any story told by Robert Morley on talk shows.

Boscastle (n.) A huge pyramid of tin cans placed just inside the entrance to a supermarket.

Boseman (n.) One who spends all day loafing about near pedestrian crossings looking as if he's about to cross.

Botley (n.) The prominent stain on a man's trouser crotch seen on his return from the bathroom. A botley proper is caused by an accident with the faucets, and should not be confused with any stain caused by insufficient waggling of the willy (see: piddletrenthide).

Botolphs (n.) Huge benign tumors that old chemistry teachers affect to wear on the sides of their noses.

Botusfleming (n. medical) A small, long-handled steel trowel used by surgeons to remove the contents of a patient's nostrils prior to a sinus operation.

Bradford (n.) A schoolteacher's old hairy jacket, now severely discolored by chalk dust, ink, egg, and the precipitations of unedifying chemical reactions.

Bradworthy (n.) One who is skilled in the art of naming loaves.

Brecon (n. anatomical term) That part of the toenail which is designed to snag on nylon stockings.

Brisbane (n.) A perfectly reasonable explanation. (Such as the one offered by a person with a gurgling cough that has nothing to do with the fact that they smoke fifty cigarettes a day.)

Broats (pl. n.) A pair of trousers with a career behind them. Broats are most commonly seen on elderly retired army officers. Originally the broats were part of their best suit back in the thirties; then in the fifties they were demoted and used for gardening. Recently, pensions not being what they were, the broats have been called out of retirement and reinstated as part of the best suit again.

Brompton (n.) A brompton is that which is said to have been committed when you are convinced you are about to blow off with a resounding trumpeting noise in a public place and all that actually slips out is a tiny "pfpt."

Bromsgrove (n.) Any urban environment containing a small amount of dog turd and about forty-five tons of bent steel pylon or a lump of concrete with holes claiming to be sculpture.
Oh, come my dear, and come with me
And wander 'neath the bromsgrove tree —Betjeman.

Brough Sowerby (n.) One who has been working at the same desk in the same office for fifteen years and has very much his own ideas about why he is continually passed over for promotion.

Brumby (n.) The fake antique plastic seal on a pretentious whisky bottle.

Brymbo (n.) The single unappetizing doughnut left in a bakery after 4:00 P.M.

Budby (n.) A nipple clearly defined through flimsy or wet material.

Bude (n.) A polite joke reserved for use in the presence of clergymen.

Buldoo (n.) A virulent red-colored pus that generally accompanies clonmult (q.v.) and sadberge (q.v.).

Burbage (n.) The sound made by an elevator filled with people all trying to breathe politely through their noses.

Bures (n. medical) The scabs on knees and elbows formed by a compulsion to make love on cheap floor matting.

Burleston (n., vb.) That peculiarly tuneless humming and whistling adopted by people who are extremely angry.

Burlingjobb (n. archaic) A seventeenth-century crime in which excrement is thrown into the street from a ground-floor window.

Burnt Yates (pl. n.) Condition to which yate (q.v.) will suddenly pass without any apparent interviewing period, after the spirit of the throckmorton (q.v.) has finally been summoned by incessant throcking (q.v.).

Burton Coggles (pl. n.) A bunch of keys found in a drawer whose purpose has long been forgotten, and which can therefore now be used only for dropping down people's backs as a cure for nosebleeds.

Burwash (n.) The pleasurable cool slosh of puddle water over the toes of your galoshes.

Caarnduncan (n.) The high-pitched and insistent cry of the young male human urging one of his peer group to do something dangerous on a cliffedge or piece of toxic-waste ground.

Cairnpat (n.) A large piece of dried dung found in mountainous terrain above the cow line, which leads the experienced tracker to believe that hikers have recently passed.

Cannock Chase (n.) In any box of chocolate-covered after-dinner mints, there are always a large number of empty envelopes and no more than four or five actual mints. The cannock chase is the process by which, no matter which part of the box you insert your fingers into, or how often, you will always extract most of the empty envelopes before pinning down an actual mint, or cannock. The cannock chase also occurs with people who put their dead matches back in the matchbox, and then embarrass themselves at parties trying to light cigarettes with three quarters of an inch of charcoal. The term is also used to describe futile attempts to pursue unscrupulous advertising agencies that steal your ideas to sell chocolates with.

Chattanooga (n.) A 1958 Chevy that is only held

together by noise, smoke, and a belief in the inalienable right of the individual to cause major accidents on the freeway.

Chenies (pl. n.) The last few sprigs or tassels of last Christmas's decorations you notice on the ceiling while lying on the sofa on an August afternoon.

Chicago (n.) The foul-smelling wind that precedes a subway train.

Chipping Ongar (n.) The disgust and embarrassment (or ongar) felt by an observer in the presence of a person festooned with kirbies (q.v.) when they don't know them well enough to tell them to wipe them off. Invariably this ongar is accompanied by an involuntary staccato twitching of the leg (or chipping).

Clabby (adj.) A clabby conversation is one struck up by a janitor or cleaning woman in order to avoid any further actual work. The opening gambit is usually designed to provoke the maximum confusion, and therefore the longest possible clabby conversation. It is vitally important to learn the correct, or clixby (q.v.), response to a clabby gambit, and not to get trapped by a ditherington (q.v.). For instance, if confronted with a clabby gambit such as "Oh, Mr. Smith, I didn't know you'd had your leg off," the ditherington response is "I haven't," whereas the clixby is "Good."

Clackavoid (n.) Technical television term for a page of dialogue from *Star Trek*.

Clackmannan (n.) The sound made by knocking over an elephant's-foot umbrella stand full of walking sticks. Hence, name for a particular kind of disco drum-riff.

Clathy (adj.) Nervously indecisive about how safely to dispose of a dud light bulb.

Clebit (n.) The silly little phone call you have to make only to say good-bye because you were cut off just as you were embarking on the harpenden (q.v.).

Clenchwarton (n. archaic) One who assists an exorcist by squeezing whichever part of the possessed the exorcist deems useful.

Clixby (adj.) Politely rude. Briskly vague. Firmly uninformative.

Clonmult (n.) A yellow ooze usually found near secretions of buldoo (q.v.) and sadberge (q.v.).

Clovis (q.v.) One who actually looks forward to putting up the Christmas decorations in the office.

Clun (n.) A leg that has gone to sleep and has to be hauled around after you.

Clunes (pl. n.) People who just won't go.

Condover (n.) One who is employed to stand about all day browsing through the magazine racks at the newsstand.

Cong (n.) Strange-shaped metal utensil found at the back of the saucepan cupboard. Many authorities believe that congs provide conclusive proof of the existence of a now extinct form of yellow vegetable that the Victorians used to boil mercilessly.

Corfe (n.) An object that is almost totally indistinguishable from a newspaper, the one crucial difference being that it belongs to somebody else and is unaccountably much more interesting than your own—which may otherwise appear to be in all respects identical. Though it is a rule of life that a train or other public place may contain any number of corfes but only one newspaper, it is quite possible to transform your own perfectly ordinary newspaper into a corfe by the simple expedient of letting somebody else read it.

Corfu (n.) The dullest person you met during the course of your holiday. Also, the only one who failed to understand that the exchanging of addresses at the end of a holiday is merely a social ritual and is absolutely not an invitation to call you or turn up unannounced on your doorstep three months later.

Corriearklet (n.) The moment at which two people, approaching from opposite ends of a long passageway, recognize each other and immediately pretend they don't. This is to avoid the ghastly embarrassment of having to *continue* recognizing each other the whole length of the corridor.

Corriecravie (n.) To avert the horrors of corrievorrie (q.v.), corriecravie is usually employed. This is the cowardly but highly skilled process by which both protagonists continue to approach while keeping up the pretense that they haven't noticed each other—by staring furiously at their feet, grimacing into a notebook, or studying the walls closely as if in a mood of deep irritation.

Corriedoo (n.) The crucial moment of false recognition in a long passageway encounter. Though both people are perfectly well aware that the other is approaching, they must eventually pretend sudden recognition. They now look up with a glassy smile, as if having spotted each other for the first time (and are *particularly* delighted to have done so), shouting out, "Haaaaallllllloooo!" as if to say: "Good grief!! You!! Here!! Of all people! Well, I never."

Corriemoillie (n.) The dreadful sinking sensation in a long passageway encounter when both protagonists immediately realize they have plumped for the corriedoo (q.v.) much too early, as they are still a good thirty yards apart. They were embarrassed by the pretense of corriecravie (q.v.) and decided to make use of the corriedoo because they felt silly. This was a mistake, as corrievorrie (q.v.) will make them seem far sillier.

Corriemuchloch (n.) Word describing the kind of person who can make a complete mess of a simple job like walking down a corridor.

Corrievorrie (n.) Corridor etiquette demands that once a corriedoo (q.v.) has been declared, corrievorrie must be employed. Both protagonists must now embellish their approach with an embarrassing combination of waving, grinning, making idiot faces, doing pirate impressions, and waggling the head from side to side while holding the other person's eyes as the smile drips off their face, until, with great relief, they pass each other.

Corstorphine (n.) A very short peremptory service held in monasteries prior to teatime to offer thanks for the benediction of digestive biscuits.

Cotterstock (n.) A piece of wood used to stir paint and thereafter stored uselessly in a shed in perpetuity.

Crail (n.) Crail is a common kind of rock or gravel. Each individual stone (due to an as yet undiscovered gravitational property) is charged with negative buoyancy. This means that no matter how much crail you remove from the garden, more of it will rise to the surface. Crail is much employed by the navy for making the paperweights and ashtrays used in submarines.

Cranleigh (n.) A mood of irrational irritation with everyone and everything.

Cromarty (n.) The brittle sludge that clings to the top of ketchup bottles and plastic tomatoes in luncheonettes.

Curry Mallet (n.) A large wooden or rubber club that poachers use to dispatch cats or other game that they can sell only to Indian restaurants. For particularly small cats the price obtainable is not worth the cost of expending ammunition.

Cushing (participial vb.) Being extra nice, doing all the dishes, buying wine, and unexpectedly cleaning out the refrigerator as a prelude to mentioning that your company is transferring you to Billings, Montana, or that you've just run over your youngest daughter.

Dalrymple (n.) Dalrymples are the things you pay extra for on pieces of handmade craftwork—the rough edges, the paint smudges, and the holes in the glazing.

Damnaglaur (n.) A certain facial expression that actors are required to demonstrate their mastery of before they are allowed to play Macbeth.

Darenth (n.) Measure = 0.0000176 mg. Defined as that amount of margarine capable of covering one hundred slices of bread to the depth of one molecule. This is the legal maximum allowed in sandwich bars in Greater London.

Deal (n.) The gummy substance found between damp toes.

Deeping St. Nicholas (n.) What streetwise kids do at Christmas. They hide on the rooftops waiting for Santa Claus so that if he arrives and goes down the chimney, they can rip off stuff from his sleigh.

Des Moines (pl. n.) The two little lines that come down from your nose.

Detchant (n.) That part of a hymn (usually a few notes at the end of a verse) where the tune goes so high or low that you suddenly have to change octaves to accommodate it.

Dewlish (adj.) (Of the hands or feet.) Prunelike after an overlong bath.

Didcot (n.) The oddly shaped bit of card that a ticket inspector cuts out of a ticket with his clipper for no apparent reason. It is a little-known fact that the confetti at Princess Margaret's wedding was made up of thousands of didcots collected by inspectors on the Royal Train.

Didling (participial vb.) The process of trying to work out who did it when reading a whodunit, and trying to keep your options open so that when you find out you can allow yourself to think that you knew perfectly well who it was all along.

Dillytop (n.) The kind of bath plug that for some unaccountable reason is actually designed to sit on top of the hole rather than fit into it.

Dipple (vb.) To try to remove a sticky something from one hand with the other, thus causing it to get stuck to the other hand and eventually to anything else you try to remove it with.

Ditherington (n.) Sudden access of panic experienced by one who realizes that he is being drawn inexorably into a clabby (q.v.) conversation; i.e., one he has no hope of enjoying, benefiting from, or understanding.

Dittisham (n.) Any music you hear on the radio to which you have to listen very carefully to determine whether it is an advertising jingle or a bona fide record. Dittishams are one of the two major reasons for the collapse of people's enthusiasm for rock. The other is Rod Stewart.

Dobwalls (pl. n.) The now hard-boiled bits of nastiness that have to be scraped off crockery by hand after it has been through a dishwasher.

Dockery (n.) Facetious behavior adopted by an accused man in the mistaken belief that this will endear him to the judge.

Dogdyke (vb.) Of dog owners, to adopt the absurd pretense that the animal shitting in the gutter has nothing to do with them.

Dolgellau (n.) The clump, or cluster, of bored, quietly enraged, mildly embarrassed men waiting for their wives to come out of a dressing room in a dress shop.

Dorchester (n.) A throaty cough by someone else so timed as to obscure the crucial part of the rather amusing remark you've just made.

Dorridge (n.) Technical term for one of the lame excuses written in very small print on the side of boxes of food to explain why there's hardly anything inside. Examples include "Contents may have settled in transit" and "To keep each biscuit fresh they have been individually wrapped in aluminum foil and cellophane and separated with corrugated lining, a cardboard flap, and heavy industrial tires."

Draffan (n.) An infuriating person who always manages to look much more dashing than anyone else by turning up unshaven and hung over at a formal party.

Drebley (n.) Name for a store that is supposed to be witty but is in fact wearisome, e.g., "The Frock Exchange," "Hair Apparent," etc.

Droitwich (n.) A street dance. The two partners approach from opposite directions and try politely to get out of each other's way. They step to the left, step to the right, apologize again, bump into each other, and repeat as often as unnecessary.

Dubuque (n.) A look given by a superior person to someone who has arrived wearing the wrong sort of shoes.

Duddo (n.) The most deformed potato in any given collection of potatoes.

Duggleby (n.) The person in front of you in the supermarket line who has just unloaded a bulging cart onto the conveyor belt and is now in the process of trying to work out which pocket they left their checkbook in, and indeed which pair of trousers.

Duleek (n.) Sudden realization, as you lie in bed waiting for the alarm to go off, that it should have gone off an hour ago.

Duluth (adj.) The smell of a taxi out of which people have just gotten.

Dunbar (n.) A highly specialized fiscal term used solely by turnstile operatives at zoos. It refers to the variable amount of increase in the admissions on a Sunday afternoon, caused by persons going to the zoo because they are in love and believe that the feeling of romance will be somehow enhanced by the smell of panther sweat and rank incontinence in the reptile house.

Dunboyne (n.) The moment of realization that the train you have just patiently watched pulling out of the station was the one you were meant to be on.

Duncraggon (n.) The name of Charles Bronson's retirement cottage.

Dungeness (n.) The uneasy feeling that the handles of the overloaded plastic supermarket bag you are carrying are getting steadily longer.

Duntish (adj.) Mentally incapacitated by a severe hangover.

East Wittering (n.) The same as west wittering (q.v.), only it's you they're trying to get away from.

Edgbaston (n.) The spare seat-cushion carried by a London bus, which is placed against the rear bumper when the driver wishes to indicate that the bus has broken down. No one knows how this charming old custom originated or how long it will continue.

Elmira (n.) Tremendously polite request made by maître d' of smart restaurant to the effect that sir might wish to put his cock back in his pants at this time.

Ely (n.) The first, tiniest inkling you get that something, somewhere, has gone terribly wrong.

Emsworth (n.) Measure of time and noiselessness, defined as the moment between the doors of an elevator's closing and its beginning to move.

Ephrata (pl. n.) Terribly embarrassing mistakes, each worse than the last and made in rapid succession.

Epping (participial vb.) The futile movements of forefingers and eyebrows used when failing to attract the attention of waiters and barmen.

Epsom (n.) An entry in a diary (such as a date or a set of initials), or a name and address in your address book, of which you haven't the faintest idea what it's doing there.

Epworth (n.) The precise value of the usefulness of epping (q.v.). It is a little-known fact that an earlier draft of the final line of the film *Gone With the Wind* had Clark Gable saying, "Frankly, my dear, I don't give an epworth," the line being eventually changed on the grounds that it might not be understood in Cleveland.

Eriboll (n.) A brown bubble of cheese containing gaseous matter that grows on Welsh rabbit. It was Sir Alexander Fleming's study of eribolls that led, indirectly, to his discovery of the fact that he didn't like Welsh rabbit very much.

Esher (n.) One of those faucets installed in public washrooms to enable the user to wash his trousers without actually getting into the basin.

Evercreech (n.) The look given by a group of polite, angry people to a rude, calm line jumper.

Ewelme (n., vb.) The smile bestowed on you by a flight attendant.

Exeter (n.) All light household and electrical goods contain a number of vital components plus at least one exeter. If you've just replaced a fuse, changed a bulb, or fixed a blender, the exeter is the small flat or round plastic piece left over, which means you have to undo everything and start all over again.

Fairymount (vb., n.) Polite word for buggery.

Farduckmanton (n. archaic) An ancient edict, mysteriously omitted from the Domesday Book, requiring that the feeding of fowl on village ponds be carried out equitably.

Farnham (n.) The feeling you get at about four o'clock in the afternoon when you haven't gotten enough done.

Farrancassidy (n.) A long and ultimately unsuccessful attempt to undo someone's bra.

Feakle (vb.) To make facial expressions similar to those that old gentlemen make to young girls in the playground.

Finuge (vb.) In any division of foodstuffs equally between several people, to give yourself the slice left over.

Fiunary (n.) The safe place you put something and then forget where it is.

Flimby (n.) One of those irritating handleless slippery translucent plastic bags you get in supermarkets, which, no matter how you hold them, always contrive to let something fall out.

Flodigarry (n. Scots) An ankle-length gabardine or oilskin tarpaulin worn by deep-sea herring fishermen in Arbroath and bartenders in Glasgow.

Foindle (vb.) To move ahead in a line very discreetly, working one's way up the line without being spotted doing so.

Forsinain (n. archaic) The right of the lord of the manor to molest dwarfs on their birthdays.

Fovant (n.) A taxi driver's gesture, a raised hand pointed out the window, which purportedly means "thank you" but actually means "fuck off out of my way."

Fraddam (n.) The small awkward-shaped piece of cheese that remains after you grate a large piece of cheese and enables you to cut your fingers.

Framlingham (n.) A kind of burglar alarm in common usage. It is cunningly designed so that it can ring at full volume in the street without apparently disturbing anyone. Other types of framlinghams are burglar alarms fitted to business premises in residential areas, which go off as a matter of routine at 5:31 P.M. on a Friday evening and do not get turned off till 9:20 A.M. on Monday morning.

Frating Green (adj.) The shade of green that is supposed to make you feel comfortable in hospitals, industrious in schools, and uneasy in police stations.

Frimley (n.) Exaggerated carefree saunter adopted by Jerry Lewis as an immediate prelude to dropping down an open manhole.

Fring (n.) The noise made by a light bulb that has just shone its last.

Frolesworth (n.) Measure. The minimum time necessary to spend frowning in deep concentration at each picture in an art gallery so everyone else doesn't think you're a complete moron.

Frosses (pl. n.) The lecherous looks exchanged between sixteen-year-olds at a party given by someone's parents.

Fulking (participial vb.) Pretending not to be in when the carol singers come around.

G

Galashiels (pl. n.) A form of particularly long sparse sideburns that are part of the mandatory uniform of British Rail guards.

Gallipoli (adj.) Of the behavior of a bottom lip trying to spit mouthwash after an injection at the dentist's. Hence, loose, floppy, useless.

Ganges (n. rare: colonial Indian) Leg rash contracted by playing too much polo. (It is a little-known fact that Prince Charles is troubled by ganges down the inside of his arms.)

Gastard (n.) Useful specially coined new word for an illegitimate child (in order to distinguish it from someone who merely carves you up on the highway, etc.).

Gildersome (adj.) Descriptive of a joke someone tells you that starts well but becomes so embellished in the telling that you start to weary of it after scarcely half an hour.

Gipping (participial vb.) The fishlike opening and closing of the jaws seen among people who have just been to the dentist and are puzzled as to whether their teeth have been put back the right way up.

Glasgow (n.) The feeling of infinite sadness engendered when walking through a place filled with happy people fifteen years younger than yourself.

Glassel (n.) A seaside pebble that was shiny and interesting when wet, and is now a lump of rock, which children nevertheless insist on filling their suitcases with at the end of a vacation.

Glemanuilt (n.) The kind of guilt that you'd completely forgotten about but that comes roaring back on your discovering an old letter in a cupboard.

Glentaggart (n.) A particular kind of tartan carryall, made exclusively under license for British Airways. When waiting to collect your luggage from an airport conveyor belt, you will notice that on the next conveyor belt along there is always a single, solitary bag going round and round uncollected. This is a glentaggart, put there by the baggage-handling staff to take your mind off the fact that your own luggage will shortly be landing in Murmansk.

Glenties (pl. n.) Series of small steps by which someone who has made a serious tactical error in a conversation or argument moves from complete disagreement to wholehearted agreement.

Glenwhilly (n. Scots) A small tartan pouch worn beneath the kilt during the thistle harvest.

Glinsk (n.) A hat that politicians buy to go to Russia in.

Glororum (n.) One who takes pleasure in informing others about his bowel movements.

Glossop (n.) A rogue blob of food. Glossops, which are generally steaming hot and highly adhesive, invariably fall off your spoon and onto the surface of your host's highly polished antique rosewood dining table. If this has not, or may not have, been noticed by the company present, swanage (q.v.) may be employed.

Glutt Lodge (n.) The place where food can be stored after a tooth is extracted. Some Arabs can go without sustenance for up to six weeks on a full glutt lodge.

Goadby Marwood (n.) Someone who stops John Cleese on the street and demands that he do a funny walk.

Godalming (n.) Wonderful rush of relief on discovering that the ely (q.v.) and the wembley (q.v.) were in fact false alarms.

Golant (adj.) Blank, sly, and faintly embarrassed. Pertaining to the expression seen on the face of someone who has clearly forgotten your name.

Goole (n.) The puddle on the bar into which the bartender puts your change.

Goosecruives (pl. n. archaic) Wooden trousers worn by poultry keepers in the Middle Ages.

Goosnargh (n.) Something left over from preparing or eating a meal, which you store in the refrigerator despite the fact that you know full well you will never ever use it.

Great Tosson (n.) A fat book containing four words and six cartoons that costs $12.95.

Great Wakering (participial vb.) Panic that sets in when you badly need to go to the bathroom and cannot make up your mind about which book or magazine to take with you.

Greeley (n.) Someone who continually annoys you by continually apologizing for annoying you.

Gretna Green (adj.) A shade of green that makes you wish you'd painted whatever it was a different color.

Grimmet (n.) A small bush from which cartoon characters dangle over the edge of a cliff.

Grimsby (n.) A lump of something gristly and foul-tasting concealed in a mouthful of stew or pie. Grimsbies are sometimes merely the result of careless cooking, but more often they are placed there deliberately by Freemasons. Grimsbies can be purchased in bulk from any respectable Masonic butcher on giving him the secret Masonic handshake. One is then put in a guest's food to see if he knows the correct Masonic method of dealing with it. If the guest is not a Mason, the host may find it entertaining to watch how he handles the obnoxious object. It may be (a) manfully swallowed, invariably bringing tears to the eyes; (b) chewed with resolution for up to twenty minutes before eventual resort to method; (c) choked on fatally.

The Masonic handshake is easily recognized by another Mason, incidentally, for by it a used grimsby is passed from hand to hand.

The secret Masonic method for dealing with a grimsby is as follows: Remove it carefully with the silver tongs provided, using the left hand. Cross the room to your host, hopping on one leg, and ram the grimsby firmly up his nose, shouting, "Take that, you smug Masonic bastard."

Grinstead (n.) The state of a woman's clothing after she has been to powder her nose and has hitched up her pantyhose over her skirt at the back, thus exposing her bottom, and walked out without noticing it.

Guernsey (adj.) Queasy but unbowed. The kind of feeling one gets when discovering that things are growing in the refrigerator.

Gweek (n.) A coat hanger recycled as a car antenna.

H

Hadzor (n.) A sharp instrument put in the kitchen sink to make it easier to cut yourself.

Hagnaby (n.) Someone who looked a lot more attractive in the disco than they do in your bed the next morning.

Halcro (n.) An adhesive fibrous cloth used to hold babies' clothes together. Thousands of tiny pieces of jam hook onto thousands of tiny pieces of dribble, enabling the cloth to become sticky.

Halifax (n.) The green synthetic Astroturf on which greengrocers display their vegetables.

Hambledon (n.) The sound of a single-engine aircraft flying by, heard while lying in a summer field, which somehow concentrates the silence and sense of space and timelessness and leaves one with a profound feeling of something or other.

Happle (vb.) To annoy people by finishing their sentences for them and then telling them what they really meant to say.

Harbledown (vb.) To maneuver a double mattress down a winding staircase.

Harbottle (n.) A particular kind of fly that lives inside double-glazed windows.

Harpenden (n.) The coda to a phone conversation, consisting of about eight exchanges, by which people try gracefully to get off the line.

Haselbury Plucknett (n.) A mechanical device for cleaning combs. It was invented during the industrial revolution at the same time as Arkwright's spinning jenny, but didn't catch on in the same way.

Hassop (n.) The pocket down the back of an armchair used for storing small coins and pieces of Lego.

Hastings (pl. n.) Things said on the spur of the moment to explain to someone who comes into a room unexpectedly precisely what it is you are doing.

Hathersage (n.) The tiny snippets of beard that coat the inside of a washbasin after shaving.

Haugham (n.) One who loudly informs other diners in a restaurant what kind of man he is by calling for the chef by his first name from the lobby.

Haxby (n.) Any garden implement found in a potting shed whose exact purpose is unclear.

Heanton Punchardon (n.) A violent argument that breaks out in the car on the way home from a party between a couple who have had to be polite to each other in company all evening.

Henstridge (n.) The dried yellow substance found between the prongs of forks in restaurants.

Herstmonceux (n.) The correct name for the gold medallion worn by someone who is in the habit of wearing his shirt open to the waist.

Hesperia (n.) Phenomenon that causes Broadway audiences to give a standing ovation to anything that moves.

Hever (n.) The panic caused by half-hearing the public address system in an airport.

Hibbing (n.) The marks left on the outside breast pocket of a storekeeper's overalls where he has attempted to put away his pen and missed.

Hickling (participial vb.) The practice of infuriating theatergoers by not only arriving late to a center-row seat, but also loudly apologizing to and patting each member of the audience in turn.

Hidcote Bartram (n.) To be caught in a hidcote bartram is to say a series of protracted and final goodbyes to a group of people, leave the house, and then realize you left your hat behind.

High Limerigg (n.) The topmost tread of a staircase, which disappears when you're climbing the stairs in the dark.

High Offley (n.) Goosnargh (q.v.) three weeks later.

Hobbs Cross (n.) The awkward leaping maneuver a woman has to go through in bed in order to make him sleep on the wet spot.

Hoddlesden (n.) An "injured" football player's limp back into the game, which draws applause but doesn't fool anybody.

Hodnet (n.) The wooden safety platform supported by scaffolding around a building under construction, from which the builders (at almost no personal risk) can drop pieces of concrete on passersby.

Hoff (vb.) To deny indignantly something that is palpably true.

Hoggeston (n.) The action of overshaking a pair of dice in a cup in the mistaken belief that this will affect the eventual outcome in your favor and not irritate everyone else.

Horton-cum-Studley (n.) The combination of little helpful grunts, nodding movements of the head, considerate smiles, upward frowns, and serious pauses that a group of people join in making in trying to elicit the next pronouncement of somebody with a dreadful stutter.

Hove (adj.) Descriptive of the expression seen on the face of one person in the presence of another who clearly isn't going to stop talking for a very long time.

Hoylake (n.) The pool of edible gravy that surrounds an

inedible and disgusting lump of meat—eaten to give the impression that the person is "just not very hungry, but mmm! this is delicious." (Peaslake is a similar experience had by vegetarians.)

Huby (n.) A half erection large enough to be a publicly embarrassing bulge in the trousers, not large enough to be of any use to anybody.

Hucknall (vb.) To crouch upward: as in the movement of a seated person's feet and legs made in order to allow a vacuum cleaner to pass beneath them.

Hull (adj.) Descriptive of the smell of a weekend cottage.

Humber (vb.) To move like the cheeks of a very fat person as the car goes over a railroad crossing.

Humby (n.) An erection that won't go down when a man has to go for a pee in the middle of making love.

Huna (n.) The result of coming to the wrong decision.

Hunsingore (n.) Medieval ceremonial brass horn with which the successful execution of an araglin (q.v.) is trumpeted from the castle battlements.

Hutlerburn (n. archaic) A burn sustained as a result of the behavior of a clumsy hutler. (The precise duties of hutlers are now lost in the mists of history.)

Huttoft (n.) The fibrous algae that grow in the dark, moist environment of trouser cuffs.

I

Ibstock (n.) Anything used to make a noise on a corrugated iron wall or picket fence by dragging it along the surface while walking past. "Mr. Bennett thoughtfully selected a stout ibstock and left the house."—Jane Austen, *Pride and Prejudice, II.*

Iping (participial vb.) The increasingly anxious shifting from leg to leg you go through when you are desperate to go to the bathroom and the person you are talking to keeps on remembering a few final things he wants to mention.

Ipswich (n.) The sound at the other end of the telephone that tells you that the automatic exchange is working very hard but is intending not actually to connect you this time, merely to let you know how difficult it is.

J

Jarrow (adj.) An agricultural device that, when towed behind a tractor, enables the farmer to spread his dung evenly across the width of the road.

Jawcraig (n. medical) A massive facial spasm brought on by being told a really astounding piece of news. A mysterious attack of jawcraig affected 40,000 sheep in Wales in 1952.

Jurby (n.) A loose woolen garment reaching to the knees and with three or more armholes, knitted by the wearer's well-meaning but incompetent aunt.

K

Kalami (n.) The ancient Eastern art of being able to refold road maps.

Kanturk (n.) An extremely intricate knot originally used for belaying the topgallant foresheets of a gaff-rigged China clipper, and now more commonly observed when trying to get an old kite out of the cupboard under the stairs.

Keele (adj.) The horrible smell caused by washing ashtrays.

Kelling (participial vb.) A person searching for something, who has reached the futile stage of looking again in all the places he has looked once already, is said to be kelling.

Kennewick (n.) Small clump of freshly plucked nostril hairs.

Kent (adj.) Politely determined not to help despite a violent urge to the contrary. Kent expressions are seen on the faces of people who are good at something watching someone else who can't do it at all.

Kentucky (adv.) Fitting exactly and satisfyingly. The

cardboard box that slides neatly into an exact space in a garage, or the last book that exactly fills a bookshelf, is said to fit "real nice and kentucky."

Kerry (n.) The small twist of skin that separates each sausage on a string.

Kettering (n.) The marks left on your bottom or thighs after sunbathing in a wicker chair.

Kettleness (adj.) The condition of not being able to pee while being watched.

Kibblesworth (n.) The amount of money by which the price of a given article in a shop is less than a sensible number, in the vain hope that at least one idiot will think it cheap. For instance, the kibblesworth on a pair of shoes priced at $49.99 is one cent.

Kimmeridge (n.) The light breeze that blows through your armpit hair when you are stretched out sunbathing.

Kingstone Bagpuise (n.) A forty-year-old 225-pound man trying to commit suicide by jogging.

Kirby (n.) Small but repulsive piece of food prominently attached to a person's face or clothing. (See also chipping ongar.)

Kirby Misperton (n.) One who kindly attempts to wipe an apparent kirby (q.v.) off another's face with a napkin, and then discovers it to be a wart or other permanent fixture, is said to have committed a kirby misperton.

Kitmurvy (n.) A man who owns all the latest sporting gadgetry and clothing (golf cart, tee cosies, ventilated shoes, Gary Player–autographed track-suit top, baseball cap, mirror sunglasses) but is still only on his second golf lesson.

Knaptoft (n.) The mysterious fluff placed in your pockets by the dry cleaners.

Kurdistan (n.) Hard stare given by a husband to his wife when he notices a sharp increase in the number of times he answers the phone to be told, "Sorry, wrong number."

L

Lackawanna (n.) The ability of a New York cabby not to know where, for instance, Central Park is.

Laconia (n.) A form of mental disorder brought on by being Dick Cavett.

Lamlash (n.) The folder on hotel dressing tables full of astoundingly dull information.

Largoward (n.) Motorists' name for the kind of pedestrian who stands beside a main road and waves on the traffic, as if it's his right-of-way.

Le Touquet (n.) A mere nothing, an unconsidered trifle, a negligible amount. Un touquet is often defined as the difference between the cost of a bottle of gin bought in a liquor store and one bought in a duty-free airport shop.

Liff (n.) A book, the contents of which are totally belied by its cover. For instance, any book whose dust jacket bears the words *This book will change your life.*

Limerigg (vb.) To jar one's leg as the result of the disappearance of a stair that isn't there in the darkness.

Lindisfarne (adj.) Descriptive of the pleasant smell of an empty cookie jar.

Listowel (n.) The small mat on the bar designed to be more absorbent than the bar, but not as absorbent as your elbows.

Little Urswick (n.) The member of any class who most inclines a teacher toward the view that capital punishment should be introduced in schools.

Llanelli (adj.) Descriptive of the waggling movement of a person's hands when shaking water from them or warming up for a piece of experimental theater.

Lochranza (n.) The long unaccompanied wail in the middle of a Scottish folk song where the pipers nip round the corner for a couple of drinks.

Longniddry (n.) Droplets that persist in running out of your nose.

Lossiemouth (n.) One of those middle-aged ladies with just a hint of a handlebar mustache.

Louth (n.) The sort of man who wears loud check jackets, has a personalized tankard behind the bar, and always gets served before you do.

Low Ardwello (n.) Seductive remark made hopefully in the back of a taxi.

Low Eggborough (n.) A quiet little unregarded man in

glasses who is building a new kind of atomic bomb in his garden shed.

Lower peover (n.) Common solution to the problem of a humby (q.v.).

Lowestoft (n.) 1. The balls of wool that collect on nice new sweaters. 2. The correct name for navel fluff.

Lowther (vb.) (Of a large group of people who have been to the cinema together.) To stand about aimlessly on the pavement and argue about whether to go and eat a Chinese meal nearby or an Indian meal at a restaurant that somebody says is very good but isn't certain where it is, or have a drink and think about it, or just go home, or have a Chinese meal nearby—until by the time agreement is reached, everything is closed.

Lubcroy (n.) The telltale little lump in the top of your swimming trunks that tells you you are going to have to spend half an hour with a safety pin trying to pull the drawstring out again.

Ludlow (n.) A wad of newspaper, folded table napkin, or lump of cardboard put under a wobbly table or chair to make it stand up straight.

Luffenham (n.) The feeling you get when the bars aren't going to be open for another forty-five minutes and the luffness (q.v.) is beginning to wear a bit thin.

Luffness (n.) The hearty feeling that comes from walking in the country with galoshes and cold ears.

Lulworth (n.) Measure of conversation. A lulworth defines the amount of the length, loudness, and embarrassment of a statement you make when everyone else in the room unaccountably stops talking at the same moment.

Luppitt (n.) The piece of leather that hangs off the bottom of your shoe before you can be bothered to get it fixed.

Lusby (n.) The fold of flesh pushing forward over the top of a bra that is too small for the woman inside it.

Luton (n.) The horseshoe-shaped rug that goes around a toilet seat.

Lybster (n., vb.) The artificial chuckle in the voice-over at the end of a supposedly funny television commercial.

Lydiard Tregoze (n.) The opposite of a mavis enderby (q.v.). An unrequited early love of your life who still causes terrible pangs though she inexplicably married a telephone repairman.

Maentwrog (n. Welsh) Celtic word for a computer spelling mistake.

Malibu (n.) The height by which the top of a wave exceeds the height to which you have rolled up your trousers.

Mankinholes (pl. n.) The small holes in a loaf of bread that give rise to the momentary suspicion that something may have made its home within.

Mapledurham (n.) A hideous piece of chipboard veneer furniture bought in a suburban furniture store and designed to hold exactly a year's supply of *National Geographics*.

Margate (n.) A margate is a particular kind of doorman who sees you every day and is on cheerful first-name terms with you, then one day refuses to let you in because you forgot your ID card.

Market Deeping (participial vb.) Stealing one piece of fruit from a fruit-and-vegetable stand.

Marlow (n.) The bottom drawer in the kitchen, the one your mother keeps paper bags in.

Marytavy (n.) A person to whom, under dire injunctions of silence, you tell a secret that you wish to be far more widely known.

Massachusetts (pl. n.) Those items and particles that people, after blowing their noses, are searching for when they look into their hankies.

Mavis Enderby (n.) The almost completely forgotten girlfriend from your distant past for whom your wife has a completely irrational jealousy and hatred.

Meath (adj.) Warm and very slightly clammy. Descriptive of the texture of your hands after the automatic drying machine has turned itself off, just damp enough to make it embarrassing if you have to shake hands with someone immediately afterward.

Meathop (n.) One who sets out for the scene of an aircraft crash with a picnic hamper.

Meeth (n.) Something that doctors will shortly tell us we are all suffering from.

Melcombe Regis (n.) The name of the style of decoration used in cocktail lounges in mock-Tudor hotels.

Mellon Udrigle (n.) The ghastly sound made by traditional folk singers.

Melton Constable (n.) A patent antiwrinkle cream that policemen wear to keep themselves looking young.

Memphis (n.) The little bits of yellow fluff that get trapped in the hinge of the windshield wipers after you polish the car with a new chamois.

Milwaukee (n.) The melodious whistling, chanting, and humming tone of the milwaukee can be heard whenever a public rest room is entered. It is the way the occupants of the cubicles have of telling you there's no lock on their door and you can't come in.

Minchinhampton (n.) The expression on a man's face when he has just zipped up his trousers without due care and attention.

Moffat (n. tailoring term) That part of your coat designed to be sat on by the person next to you on the bus.

Molesby (n.) The kind of family that drives to the country and then sits in the car with all the windows closed, reading the Sunday newspapers and wearing sidcups (q.v.).

Monkstoft (n.) The bundle of hair that is left after a monk has been tonsured, which he keeps tied up with a rubber band and uses for chasing ants away.

Motspur (n.) The fourth wheel of a supermarket cart, which looks identical to the other three but renders the cart completely uncontrollable.

Mugeary (n. medical) The substance from which the

unpleasant little yellow globules in the corners of a sleepy person's eyes are made.

Munderfield (n.) A meadow selected, while driving past, as being ideal for a picnic, which, from a sitting position, turns out to be full of stubble, dust, and cow pats, and almost impossible to enjoy yourself in.

Naas (n.) The wine-making region of Albania where most of the wine that people take to bring-your-own-bottle parties comes from.

Nacton (n.) The *'n'* with which cheap advertising copy-writers replace the word *and* (as in "fish 'n' chips," "mix 'n' match," "assault 'n' battery"), in the mistaken belief that this is in some way chummy or endearing.

Nad (n.) 1 nad = 18.4 cm. Measure defined as the distance between a driver's outstretched fingertips and the ticket machine in a parking lot.

Nanhoron (n. medical) A tiny valve concealed in the inner ear that enables a deaf grandmother to converse quite normally when she feels like it, but excludes completely anything that sounds like a request to help with setting the table.

Nantucket (n.) The secret pocket that eats your train ticket.

Nantwich (n.) A late-night snack, invented by the Earl of Nantwich, which consists of the dampest thing in the refrigerator pressed between two of the driest things in the refrigerator. The earl invented the nantwich to avoid having to go shopping.

Naples (pl. n.) The tiny depressions in an English muffin.

Naseby (n.) The stout metal instrument used for clipping labels onto exhibits at flower shows.

Nashua (n.) Feeling of miserable dissatisfaction that American Express hopes you will suffer from after reading one of their "executive living" magazines.

Naugatuck (n.) A plastic packet containing shampoo, ketchup, etc., which is impossible to open except by biting off the corners.

Nazeing (participial vb.) The rather unconvincing noises of pretended interest that an adult has to make when brought a small dull object for admiration, by a child.

Neen Sollars (pl. n.) Any ensemble of especially unflattering and peculiar garments worn by a woman that tells you that she is right at the forefront of fashion.

Nempnett Thrubwell (n.) The feeling experienced when driving off for the first time on a brand-new motorcycle.

Nottage (n.) Nottage is the collective name for things that you find a use for immediately after you've thrown them away. For instance, your greenhouse has been cluttered up for years with a huge piece of cardboard and great fronds of gardening string. You at last decide to clear all this stuff out, and you burn it. Within twenty-four hours you will urgently need to wrap a large parcel, and suddenly remember that luckily in your greenhouse there is some cardb. . .

Nubbock (n.) The kind of person who has to leave a party before everyone can relax and enjoy himself.

Nutbourne (n.) In a choice between two or more possible desserts, the one nobody opts for.

Nybster (n.) The sort of person who takes the elevator to travel one floor.

Ockle (n.) An electrical switch that appears to be off in both positions.

Osbaston (n.) A point made for the seventh time to somebody who insists that they know exactly what you mean but clearly hasn't got the faintest idea.

Oshkosh (n., vb.) The noise made by someone who has just been grossly flattered and is trying to make light of it.

Ossett (n.) A frilly spare-toilet-roll cosy.

Oswaldtwistle (n. Old Norse) Small brass wind instrument used for summoning Vikings to lunch when they're off on their longships playing.

Oswestry (abs. n.) Bloody-minded determination on the part of a storyteller to continue a story that both the teller and the listeners know has become desperately tedious.

Oughterby (n.) Someone you don't want to invite to a party but whom you know you have to as a matter of duty.

Oundle (vb.) To walk along leaning sideways, with one

arm hanging limp and dragging one leg behind the other. Most commonly used by actors in amateur productions of *Richard III*, or by people carrying a heavy suitcase in one hand.

Ozark (n.) One who offers to help just after all the work has been done.

Pabbay (n., vb.) (Fencing term.) The play, or maneuver, where one swordsman leaps onto the table and pulls the battle-ax off the wall.

Pant-y-Wacco (adj.) The final state of mind of a retired colonel before they come to take him away.

Papcastle (n.) Something drawn or modeled by a small child, and you are supposed to know what it is.

Papple (vb.) To do what babies do to soup with their spoons.

Papworth Everard (n.) Technical term for the third take of an orgasm scene during the making of a pornographic film.

Peebles (pl. n.) Small, carefully rolled pellets of skegness (q.v.).

Pelutho (n.) A South American ball game. The balls are whacked against a brick wall with a stout wooden bat until the prisoner confesses.

Penge (n.) The expanding slotted arm on which a cuckoo comes out of a cuckoo clock.

Pen-tre-tafarn-y-fedw (n.) Welsh word that literally translates as "leaking-ballpoint-by-the-glass-hole-of-the-clerk-of-the-bank-has-been-taken-to-another-place-leaving-only-the-special-inkwell-and-three-inches-of-tin-chain."

Peoria (n.) The fear of peeling too few potatoes.

Perranzabuloe (n.) One of those spray things used to wet ironing.

Piddletrenthide (n.) A trouser stain caused by a wimbledon (q.v.). Not to be confused with a botley (q.v.).

Pimlico (n.) Small odd-shaped piece of plastic or curious metal component found in the bottom of a kitchen drawer in the course of spring cleaning or looking for Scotch tape.

Pimperne (n.) One of those rubber nodules found on the underneath side of a toilet seat.

Pitlochry (n.) The background gurgling noise heard at McDonald's, caused by people trying to get the last bubbles out of their milk shakes by slurping loudly through their straws.

Pitsligo (n.) Part of traditional mating rite. During the first hot day of spring, all the men in the subway start giving up their seats to women and straphanging. The purpose of pitsligo is for them to demonstrate their manhood by displaying the wet patches under their arms.

Pleeley (adj.) Descriptive of a drunk person's attempts to be endearing.

Plymouth (vb.) To relate an amusing story to someone without remembering that it was they who told it to you in the first place.

Plympton (n.) The (pointless) knob on top of a war memorial.

Poges (pl. n.) The lumps of dry powder that remain after cooking an instant soup.

Polbathic (adj.) Gifted with the ability to manipulate water faucets using only the feet.

Polloch (n.) One of those tiny ribbed-plastic and aluminum-foil containers of milk served on trains, enabling you to carry one safely back to your compartment, where you can spill the contents all over your legs in comfort trying to get the bloody thing open.

Polperro (n.) A polperro is the ball of soggy hair found clinging to bathtub drains.

Ponka City (n.) An elevator full of immensely fat people in sweat shirts.

Poona (n.) Satisfied grunting noise made when sitting back after a good meal.

Pott Shrigley (n.) Dried remains of a week-old casserole, eaten when extremely drunk at 2:00 A.M.

Pudsey (n.) The curious-shaped flat wads of dough left on a kitchen table after someone has been cutting cookies out.

Quabbs (pl. n.) The substance that emerges when you squeeze a blackhead.

Quall (vb.) To speak with the voice of one who requires another to do something for them.

Quedgeley (n.) A rabidly left-wing politician who can afford to be that way because he married a millionairess.

Quenby (n.) A stubborn spot on a window that you spend twenty minutes trying to clean off before discovering it's on the other side of the glass.

Querrin (n.) A person that no one has ever heard of who unaccountably manages to make a living writing prefaces.

Quoyness (n.) The hatefulness of words like *relionus* and *easiephit*.

R

Ramsgate (n.) All institutional buildings must, by law, contain at least twenty ramsgates. These are doors that open the opposite way to the one you expect.

Ranfurly (adj.) The fashion of tying ties so that the long thin end underneath dangles below the short fat upper end.

Ripon (vb.) (Of literary critics.) To include all the best jokes from the book in review to make it look as if the critic thought of them.

Rochester (n.) One who is able to gain occupation of the armrests on both sides of a movie theater or airplane seat.

Royston (n.) The man behind you in church who sings with terrific gusto almost three quarters of a tone off the note.

S

Sadberge (n.) A violent green shrub that is ground up, mixed with twigs and gelatin, and served with clonmult (q.v.) and buldoo (q.v.) in a container referred to for no known reason as a "relish tray."

Saffron Walden (n.) A particular kind of hideous casual jacket that nobody wears in real life, but is much favored by Doc Severinsen.

Satterthwaite (vb.) To spray the person you are talking to with half-chewed bread crumbs.

Savernake (vb.) To sew municipal crests on a Windbreaker in the belief that this will make the wearer appear cosmopolitan.

Scamblesby (n.) A small dog that resembles a throw rug and appears to be dead.

Scethrog (n.) One of those peculiar beards-without-mustaches worn by religious Belgians and American scientists, which make them look like trolls.

Sconser (n.) A person who looks around when talking to you, to see if there's anyone more interesting about.

Scopwick (n.) The flap of skin that is torn off your lip when you smoke an unfiltered cigarette.

Scorrier (n.) A small hunting dog trained to snuffle among your private parts.

Scosthrop (vb.) To make vague opening or cutting movements with the hands when wandering about looking for a can opener, scissors, etc., in the hope that this will help in some way.

Scottsbluff (n.) One who frowns at his newly lit cigarette.

Scrabby (n.) A curious-shaped dustcloth given to you by your mother that on closer inspection turns out to be half of a pair of underpants.

Scrabster (n.) A dog that mounts your leg during tea.

Scramoge (vb.) To cut oneself while licking envelopes.

Scranton (n.) A person who, after the declaration of the bodmin (q.v.), always says, "But I only had the tomato soup."

Scraptoft (n.) The absurd flap of hair a vain and balding man grows long above one ear to comb plastered over the top of his head to the other ear.

Screeb (n.) To make the noise of a nylon parka rubbing against a pair of corduroy trousers.

Screggan (n. banking) The crossing-out caused by people putting the wrong year on their checks all through January.

Scremby (n.) The dehydrated felt-tip pen attached by a string to the "Don't Forget" board in the kitchen, which has never worked in living memory but which no one can be bothered to throw away.

Scroggs (n.) The stout pubic hairs that protrude from your moussaka in a cheap Greek restaurant.

Scronkey (n.) Something that hits the window as the result of a violent sneeze.

Scullet (n.) The last teaspoon in the dirty dishes.

Seattle (vb.) To make a noise like a train going along.

Seminole (n.) Congealed deposits found deep inside a woonsocket (q.v.).

Shalunt (n.) One who wears Trinidad and Tobago T-shirts on the beach in Bali to prove they didn't just win the holiday in a competition or anything.

Shanklin (n.) The hoop of skin around a single slice of salami.

Shenandoah (n.) The infinite smugness of those who know they are entitled to a place in a nuclear bunker.

Sheppey (n.) Measure of distance (equal to approximately seven eighths of a mile), defined as the closest distance at which sheep remain picturesque.

Shifnal (n., vb.) An awkward shuffling walk caused by two or more people in a hurry accidentally getting into the same segment of a revolving door. A similar effect is achieved by people entering three-legged races unwisely joined at the neck instead of the ankles.

Shirmers (pl. n.) Tall young men who stand around smiling at weddings as if to suggest that they know the bride rather well.

Shoeburyness (abs. n.) The vague uncomfortable feeling you get when sitting on a seat that is still warm from somebody else's bottom.

Shrivenham (n.) One of Germaine Greer's used-up lovers.

Sidcup (n.) One of those hats made from tying knots in the corners of a handkerchief.

Silesia (n. medical) The inability to remember, at the critical moment, which is the better side of a boat to be seasick off.

Silloth (n.) Something that was sticky, and is now furry, found on the carpet under the sofa the morning after a party.

Simprim (n.) The little movement of false modesty by

which a woman with a cavernous visible cleavage pulls her skirt down over her knees.

Sittingbourne (n.) One of those conversations where both people are waiting for the other one to shut up so they can get on with their bit.

Skegness (n.) Nose excreta of a malleable consistency.

Skellow (adj.) Descriptive of the satisfaction experienced when looking at a really good dry-stone wall.

Skenfrith (n.) The flakes of athlete's foot found inside socks.

Sketty (n.) Apparently self-propelled little dance a beer glass performs in its own puddle.

Skibbereen (n.) The noise made by a sunburned thigh leaving a plastic chair.

Sligo (n.) An unnamed and exotic sexual act that people like to believe that famous film stars get up to in private, as in "to commit sligo."

Slogarie (n.) Hill-walking dialect for the seven miles of concealed rough moorland that lie between what you thought was the top of the hill and what actually is.

Slubbery (n.) The gooey drips of wax that dribble down the sides of a candle, so beloved by Italian restaurants with Chianti bottles.

Sluggan (n.) A lurid facial bruise that everyone politely omits to mention because it's obvious that you had a fight with your spouse last night—but that was actually caused by walking into a door. It is useless to volunteer the true explanation, because nobody will believe it.

Slumbay (n.) The cigarette butt someone discovers in the mouthful of beer they have just swigged from a can at the end of a party.

Smarden (vb.) To keep your mouth shut by smiling determinedly through your teeth. Smardening is largely used by people trying to give the impression that they're enjoying a story they've heard at least six times before.

Smearisary (n.) That part of a kitchen wall reserved for the finger paintings of small children.

Smisby (n.) The correct name for a junior apprentice greengrocer whose main duty is to arrange the fruit so that the bad side is underneath. From the name of a character not in Dickens.

Sneem (n., vb.) Particular kind of frozen smile bestowed on a small child by a parent in mixed company when the question "Mommy, what's this?" appears to require the answer, "Er... it's a rubber, darling."

Snitter (n.) One of the rather unfunny newspaper clippings pinned to an office wall, the humor of which is supposed to derive from the fact that the headline contains a name similar to that of one of the occupants of the office.

Snitterby (n.) Someone who pins a snitter (q.v.) on a snitterfield (q.v.).

Snitterfield (n.) Office bulletin on which snitters (q.v.) pin cards saying, "You don't have to be crazy to work here, but it helps!!!" and slightly smutty postcards from Ibiza get pinned up by snitterbies (q.v.).

Snohomish (adj.) Descriptive of the feeling experienced at the end of a Hollywood party, when everything has been consumed and you just want to be in bed for a few days.

Solent (adj.) Descriptive of the state of serene self-knowledge reached through drink.

Sotterley (n.) Uncovered area between two shops with awnings, which you have to cross when it's raining.

Spittal of Glenshee (n.) That which has to be cleaned off castle floors in the morning after a bagpipe contest or vampire attack.

Spofforth (vb.) To tidy up a room before the cleaning woman arrives.

Stebbing (n.) The erection you cannot conceal because you're not wearing a jacket.

Stoke Poges (n.) The tapping movements of an index finger on glass made by a person futilely attempting to communicate with *either* a tropical fish *or* a post-office clerk.

Sturry (n., vb.) A token run. Pedestrians who have chosen to cross a road immediately in front of an approaching vehicle generally give a little wave and break into a sturry. This gives the impression of hurrying without having any practical effect whatsoever on their speed.

Sutton and Cheam (nouns) Sutton and cheam are the two kinds of dirt into which all dirt is divided. Sutton is the dark sort that always gets on light-colored things, and cheam the light-colored sort that clings to dark items. Anyone who has ever found seagull goo on a dinner jacket (a) knows all about sutton and cheam, and (b) is going to some very curious dinner parties.

Swanage (pl. n.) Swanage is the series of diversionary tactics used when trying to cover up the existence of a glossop (q.v.) and may include (a) uttering a high-pitched laugh and pointing out the window (NB: This doesn't work more than twice); (b) sneezing as loudly as possible and wiping the glossop off the table in the same movement as whipping out your handkerchief; (c) saying "Christ! I seem to have dropped some shit on your table" (very unwise); (d) saying, "Christ, who did that?" (better); (e) pressing your elbow onto the glossop itself and working your arms slowly to the edge of the table; (f) leaving the glossop where it is but moving a plate over it and putting up with sitting at an uncomfortable angle the rest of the meal; or, if the glossop is in too exposed a position; (g) leaving it there unremarked except for the occasional humorous glance.

Swanibost (adj.) Completely wiped out after a hard day having the income tax code explained to you.

Symond's Yat (n.) The little spoonful inside the lid of a recently opened boiled egg.

T

Tabley Superior (n.) The look directed at you in a theater bar in the intermission by people who've already got their drinks.

Tampa (n.) The sound of a rubber eraser coming to rest after dropping off a desk in a very quiet room.

Taroom (vb.) To make loud noises during the night to let the burglars know you are in.

Tegucigalpa (n.) An embarrassing mistake arising out of confusing the shape of something rather rude with something perfectly ordinary when groping for it in the darkness. A common example of a tegucigalpa is when a woman pulls a packet of tampons out of her bag and offers them around under the impression that they are cigarettes.

Theakstone (n.) Ancient mad tramp who jabbers to himself and swears loudly and obscenely on station platforms and traffic islands.

Throcking (participial vb.) (1) The action of continually pushing down the lever on a pop-up toaster in the hope that you will thereby get it to understand that you want it to toast something. (2) A style of drum playing

87

favored by Nigel Olsson of the Elton John Band, reminiscent of the sound of someone slapping a frankfurter against a bucket. An excellent example of this is to be heard on "Someone Saved My Life Tonight" from the album *Captain Fantastic and the Brown Dirt Cowboy*.

Throckmorton (n.) The soul of a departed madman: one of those now known to inhabit the timing mechanism of pop-up toasters.

Thrumster (n.) The irritating man next to you in a concert who thinks he's (a) the conductor, (b) the brass section.

Thrupp (vb.) To hold one end of a ruler on a desk and make the other end go bbddbbddbbrrbrrrddrr.

Thurnby (n.) A turned-up edge of carpet or linoleum that everyone says someone will trip over and break a leg unless it gets fixed. After a year or two someone trips over it and breaks a leg.

Tibshelf (n.) Crisscross wooden construction hung on a wall in a teenage girl's bedroom, covered with glass Bambis and poodles, matching pigs, and porcelain ponies in various postures.

Tidpit (n.) The corner of a toenail, from which satisfying little black deposits may be sprung.

Tigharry (n.) The shill who gets unsuspecting people to participate in three-card monte games by winning an improbable amount of money very easily.

Tillicoultry (n.) The man-to-man chumminess adopted by an employer as a prelude to telling an employee that he's going to have to let him go.

Timble (vb.) (Of small nasty children.) To fall over very gently, look around to see who's about, and then yell blue murder.

Tincleton (n.) A man who amuses himself in your bathroom by pulling the chain or pressing the handle in mid-pee and then seeing if he can finish before the flush does.

Tingrith (n.) The feeling of aluminum foil against your fillings.

Todber (n.) One whose idea of a good time is to stand behind his front hedge and give surly nods to people he doesn't know.

Todding (vb.) The business of talking amiably and aimlessly to bartenders.

Tolob (n.) A crease or fold in an underblanket, the removal of which involves getting out of bed and largely remaking it.

Tolstachaolais (phr.) What the police require you to say in order to prove that you are not drunk.

Tooting Bec (n.) A car behind which one draws up at the traffic lights and honks at when the lights turn green before realizing that the car is parked and there is no one inside.

Torlundy (n.) Narrow but thickly grimed strip of floor between the refrigerator and the sink unit in the kitchen of a rented apartment.

Toronto (n.) Generic term for anything that comes out in a gush despite all your careful efforts to let it out gently; e.g., flour into a white sauce, tomato ketchup onto fried fish, sperm into a human being., etc.

Totteridge (n.) The ridiculous two-inch hunch that people adopt when arriving late for the theater in the vain and futile hope that it will minimize either their embarrassment or the lack of visibility for the rest of the audience. (Cf. hickling.)

Trantlemore (vb.) To make a noise like a train crossing a set of points.

Trewoofe (n.) A very thick and heavy drift of snow balanced precariously on the edge of a door porch waiting for what it judges to be the correct moment to fall. From the ancient Greek legend "The Trewoofe of Damocles."

Trispen (n.) A form of intelligent grass. It grows a single, tough stalk and makes its home on lawns. When it sees the lawn mower coming it lies down, and pops up again after it has gone by.

Trossachs (pl. n.) The useless epaulettes on an expensive raincoat.

Tuamgraney (n.) A hideous wooden ornament that people hang over the mantelpiece to prove they've been to Africa.

Tulsa (n.) A slurp of beer that has accidentally gone down your shirt collar.

Tumby (n.) The involuntary abdominal gurgling that fills the silence following someone else's intimate personal revelation.

Tweedsmuir (collective n.) The name given to the extensive collection of hats kept in the downstairs bathroom that don't fit anyone in the family.

Twomileborris (n.) A popular East European outdoor game in which the first person to reach the front of the line at the butcher's wins, and the losers have to forfeit their bath plugs.

Tyne and Wear (nouns) The tyne is the small priceless or vital object accidentally dropped on the floor (e.g., diamond tie clip, contact lens), and the wear is the large immovable object (e.g., dresser, car) that it hides under.

Ullapool (n.) The spittle that builds up on the floor of the orchestra pit.

Ullingswick (n.) An overdeveloped epiglottis found in middle-aged coloraturas.

Ullock (n.) The correct name for either of the deaf Scandinavian tourists who are standing two abreast in front of you on the escalator.

Umberleigh (n.) The awful movement that follows a dorchester (q.v.) when a speaker decides whether to repeat an amusing remark after nobody laughed the last time. To be on the horns of an umberleigh is to wonder whether people didn't hear the remark, or whether they did hear it and just didn't think it was funny, which was why somebody coughed.

Upottery (n.) That part of a kitchen cupboard that contains an unnecessarily large number of milk jugs.

Uttoxeter (n.) A small but immensely complex mechanical device that is essentially the brain of a modern coffee-vending machine, enabling the machine to make its own decisions.

Valletta (n.) An ornate headdress or loose garment worn by a person in the belief that it renders him or her invisibly native and not like a tourist at all. People who don huge conical straw coolie hats with "I Luv Lagos" on them in Nigeria, and tourists in Malaya who insist on appearing in the hotel lobby wearing a sarong, know what we're talking about.

Vancouver (n.) The technical name for one of those huge trucks with whirling brushes on the bottom, used to clean streets.

Ventnor (n.) One who, having been visited as a child by a mysterious gypsy lady, is gifted with the strange power of being able to operate the air nozzles above airplane seats.

Vobster (n.) A strain of perfectly healthy rodents that develop cancer the moment they enter a laboratory.

Warleggan (n. archaic) One who does not approve of araglins (q.v.).

Warwarsing (participial vb.) A kind of heavy, prancing, wallowing movement made by New York cabs going up Eighth Avenue and being careful not to avoid potholes.

Weem (n.) The tool with which a dentist can inflict the greatest pain. Formerly, which tool this was was dependent upon the imagination and skill of the individual dentist, though now, with technological advances, weems can be bought specially.

Wembley (n.) The hideous moment of confirmation that the diaster presaged in the ely (q.v.) has actually struck.

West Wittering (participial vb.) The uncontrollable twitching that breaks out when you're trying to get away from the most boring person at a party.

Wetwang (n.) A moist penis.

Whaplode Drove (n.) A homicidal golf stroke.

Whasset (n.) A business card in your wallet belonging to someone whom you have no recollection of meeting.

Whissendine (n.) The noise that occurs (often at night) in a strange house, which is too short and too irregular for you ever to be able to find out what it is and where it comes from.

Wigan (n.) If, when talking to someone who you know has only one leg, you're trying to treat them perfectly casually and normally, but find to your horror that your conversation is liberally studded with references to Long John Silver, Hopalong Cassidy, "putting your foot in it," "the last leg of the marathon," you are said to have committed a wigan.

Wike (vb.) To rip an adhesive bandage off your skin as fast as possible in the hope that it will (a) show how brave you are, and (b) not hurt.

Willimantic (adj.) Of a person whose heart is in the wrong place (i.e., between their legs).

Wimbledon (n.) That last drop, which, no matter how much you shake it, always goes down your trouser leg.

Winkley (n.) A lost object that turns up immediately after you've gone and bought a replacement for it.

Winston-Salem (n.) A person in a restaurant who suggests to his companions that they should split the cost of the meal equally, and then orders two packs of cigarettes on the bill.

Wivenhoe (n.) The cry of alacrity with which a sprightly eighty-year-old breaks the ice on the lake when going for a swim on Christmas Eve.

Woking (participial vb.) Standing in the kitchen wondering what you came in here for.

Woolfardisworthy (n.) A mumbled, mispronounced, or misheard word in a song, speech, or play. Derived from the well-known mumbled passage in *Hamlet*:
> . . . and the spurns,
> That patient merit of the unworthy takes
> When he himself might his quietus make
> With a bare bodkin? Who woolfardisworthy
> To grunt and sweat under a weary life?

Woonsocket (n.) A knothole in a tree in a very secluded part of Central Park.

Worgret (n.) A kind of poltergeist that specializes in stealing road maps from your car.

Worksop (n.) A person who never actually gets around to doing anything because he spends all his time writing out lists headed "Things to Do (Urgent)."

Wormelow tump (n.) Any seventeen-year-old who doesn't know about anything at all other than bicycle gears.

Wrabness (n.) The feeling after having tried to dry oneself with a damp towel.

Writtle (vb.) Of a steel ball, to settle into a hole.

Wroot (n.) A short little jerk who thinks that by pulling on his pipe and gazing shrewdly at you he will give the impression that he is infinitely wise and five feet eleven inches tall.

Wyoming (participial vb.) Moving in hurried desperation from one cubicle to another in a public lavatory, trying to find one that has a lock on the door, a seat on the bowl, and no brown streaks on the seat.

Yakima (n.) Ancient Japanese term for the very special courage required to pluck sensitive young nostril hairs.

Yarmouth (vb.) To shout at foreigners in the belief that the louder you speak, the better they'll understand you.

Yate (n.) Dishearteningly white piece of bread that sits limply in a pop-up toaster during a protracted throcking (q.v.) session.

Yesnaby (n.) A "yes, maybe" that means "no."

Yonder Bognie (n.) The kind of restaurant, advertised as "just three minutes from the movie theater," which clearly nobody ever goes to, and, even if they had ever contemplated it, have certainly changed their mind since seeing the ad.

Yonkers (n.) (Rare.) The combined thrill of pain and shame when being caught in public plucking your nostril hairs and stuffing them into your pocket.

York (vb.) To shift the position of the shoulder straps on a heavy bag or knapsack in a vain attempt to make it seem lighter. Hence, to laugh falsely and heartily at an unfunny remark. "Jasmine yorked politely, loathing him to the depths of her being."—Virginia Woolf.

Yuba (n.) Intelligence test that applicants are required to fail before they can be considered for the position of bank teller.

Z

Zeal Monachorum (n.) (Skiing term.) To ski with zeal monachorum is to descend the top three quarters of the mountain in a quivering blue funk, but on arriving at the gentle bit just in front of the restaurant to whizz to a stop like a victorious slalom champion.

Zebulon (n.) A New York crazy who quite genuinely is from another planet, but who's ever going to believe him?

INDEX OF MEANINGS

bags
  paper, maternal: *Marlow*
  slippery, translucent: *Flimby*
  solitary, Scottish: *Glentaggart*
  supermarket: *Dungeness*
bakers: *Bradworthy, Brymbo*
baldness: *Scraptoft*
ballads, raucous old: *Banteer*
ballpoints, leaky: *Pen-tre-tafarn-y-fedw*
balls
  soggy, hairy; *Polperro*
  steel: *Writtle*
bamboo: *Blitterlees*
bands
  rock: *Dittisham, Throcking*
  rubber: *Monkstoft*
banks: *Albuquerque, Pen-tre-tafarn-y-fedw, Screggan, Yuba*
bars
  jerks in: *Boothby Graffoe, Louth*
  waiting for the, to open: *Luffenham*
  wet: *Listowel*
bartenders
  aimless: *Todding*
  surly: *Goole*
bastards
  bloody rude: *Fovant*
  inconsiderate, stupid, filthy: *Dogdyke*
  in technical sense: *Gastard*
  lazy: *Abinger, Ozark*
  mad and/or lazy: *Boseman*
  six-year-old: *Little Urswick*
  smooth, beery: *Louth*
  smooth, lecherous, young: *Shirmers*
  smug, self-important, old: *Shenandoah*
  smug, shitty, Masonic: *Grimsby*
  vile, vain, rich: *Shalunt*

baths
  prunelike objects in: *Dewlish*
  round, rubbery objects in: *Dillytop*
bats
  hairy, harmless old: *Lossiemouth*
  incompetent, well-meaning old: *Jurby*
  stout, wooden: *Pelutho*
battle-axes, sharp, on castle wall: *Pabbay*
bbddbbddbbrrbrrrrddrr, things that go: *Thrupp*
beating: *Aboyne*
bed
  area to be avoided in: *Hobbs Cross*
  banana-shaped object on: *Baumber*
  dreadful mistakes in: *Hagnaby*
  things found in: *Ballycumber*
  things that jump out of: *Duleek*
  unwelcome lumps in: *Tolob*
bedrooms, other people's: *Beaulieu Hill, Tibshelf*
behavior, facetious, misguided: *Dockery*
behind
  dragging one leg: *Oundle*
  leaving one's hat: *Hidcote Bartram*
Belgians, hairy, religious: *Scethrog*
beliefs, mistaken, humorous: *Dockery*
bicycle gears: *Wormelow Tump*
birthdays, dwarfish: *Forsinain*
biscuits, digestive, religious: *Corstorphine*
blobs
  bloody-minded: *Glossop*

stubborn: *Quenby*
bloody murder: *Timble*
blue funk: *Zeal Monachorum*
boards, "Don't Forget": *Scremby*
bodkins, bare: *Woolfardisworthy*
book reviews: *Ripon*
books
  bathroom: *Great Wakering*
  fat, expensive: *Great Tosson*
  various: *Ballycumber*
  very deceptive: *Liff*
bookshelves: *Ahenny*
bores
  pompous, any age: *Ardcrony*
  worst, at party: *West Wittering*
bottle parties: *Aasleagh*
bottles
  gin: *Le Touquet*
  ketchup: *Cromarty*
  whisky: *Brumby*
bottom
  huge whirling brushes on:
    Vancouver
  interesting patterns on own:
    Kettering
  of shoes: *Luppitt*
  warmth of other people's:
    Shoeburyness
bottom drawers: *Marlow*
bottom exposed: *Grinstead*
bottom lip: *Gallipoli*
bottom sheet: *Baumber, Bedfont*
boxes
  in garages: *Kentucky*
  things upside down in: *Bolsover*
brain, of coffee machine:
  Uttoxeter
bras
  impossible: *Farrancassidy*
  inadequate: *Lusby*
bread
  hundred slices of: *Darenth*
  single slice of: *Yate*

wildlife in: *Mankinholes*
bread crumbs, half-chewed:
  Satterthwaite
breezes, in armpit: *Kimmeridge*
bring-your-own-bottle: *Naas*
bristles: *Aith*
Bronson, Charles: *Duncraggon*
browser, vertical: *Condover*
bruises, lurid, accidental:
  Sluggan
bubbles
  congealed, cheesy: *Eriboll*
  slurped, milky: *Pitlochry*
buggery: *Fairymount*
builders, murderous: *Hodnet*
bulbs, light: *Fring*
bulges
  cheesy: *Eriboll*
  dealing with: *Lower Peover*
  huge, benign: *Botolphs*
  huge, erotic: *Humby*
  medium-sized, erotic: *Huby*
  prestressed: *Bromsgrove*
  pustular: *Bilbster*
  tiny, erotic: *Budby*
  unwelcome, obvious: *Stebbing*
bunches, usless: *Burton Coggles*
bunkers, nuclear: *Shenandoah*
burglars: *Taroom*
burns, nonpoetic: *Hutlerburn*
buses
  desire on: *Abercrave*
  oversized: *Articlave*
  parts of: *Edgbaston*
  parts on: *Moffat*
bushes, small, humorous:
  Grimmet
buttons
  bacony: *Beccles*
  belly: *Lowestoft*

cafés, nasty: *Cromarty*
camera stores: *Ainsworth*

candles, deformed: *Slubbery*
cans, tin: *Boscastle*
carol singers, avoidance of: *Fulking*
carpet, turned-up edges of: *Thurnby*
cartoons
  sparing use of: *Great Tosson*
  vegetation in: *Grimmet*
cats, methods of dispatching: *Curry Mallet*
cavities
  definitely unhygienic: *Glutt Lodge, Henstridge*
  probably unhygienic: *Mankinholes*
Cavett, Dick: *Laconia*
Central Park: *Lackawanna, Seminole, Woonsocket*
chairs
  dismantled: *Blitterlees*
  plastic, sweaty: *Skibbereen*
  wicker: *Kettering*
chambermaids, embarrassing discoveries of: *Bedfont*
change
  small: *Boolteens*
  small, wet: *Goole*
Charles, Prince: *Ganges*
cheese, cottage: *Berkhamsted*
cheese graters: *Abinger*
cheese, various sizes of: *Fraddam*
chef, loudmouths who call for the: *Haugham*
chess: *Bishop's Caundle*
Chevrolet: *Chattanooga*
chewing gum: *Belper*
children, small
  inconvenient: *Glassel*
  rude, innocent: *Sneem*
  untidy: *Smearisary*
  untalented: *Papcastle*

  yelling: *Timble*
chimney, coming down the: *Deeping St. Nicholas*
chocolates: *Bolsover, Cannock Chase*
chuckles, chummy: *Lybster*
chumminess, man-to-man: *Tillicoultry*
cigarette butts, in beer: *Slumbay*
cigarettes
  frowns at: *Scottsbluff*
  two packs of: *Winston-Salem*
  unfiltered: *Scopwick*
Claus, Santa: *Deeping St. Nicholas*
cleaning, dry: *Knaptoft*
cleaning women: *Spofforth*
cleavages, speleological, monstrous: *Simprim*
Cleese, John: *Goadby Marwood*
cliff edges, silly little kids on: *Caarnduncan*
clippers, gaff-rigged China: *Kanturk*
clocks
  alarm: *Duleek*
  cuckoo: *Penge*
clubs, rubber: *Curry Mallet*
codgers
  boring, famous: *Boothby Graffoe*
  huge, wobbling, wheezing, old: *Kingston Bagpuise*
  stuffy, medieval, old: *Warleggan*
  twinkly, disgusting, old: *Feakle*
coffee machines, intelligent: *Uttoxeter*
combs, clogged: *Haselbury Plucknett*
components
  small, meaningless; *Pimlico*
  vital, missing: *Exeter*
confetti, royal: *Didcot*

conversations
  interminable: *Ditherington*
  polite, interminable: *Clabby*
  polite, pointless: *Sittingbourne*
  shifting: *Glenties*
  wasted: *Harpenden*
cookie jars: *Lindisfarne*
cookies: *Pudsey*
corners, biting off: *Naugatuck*
cosies, spare-toilet-roll: *Ossett*
cottages
  retirement: *Duncraggon*
  weekend: *Hull*
coughs
  gurgling: *Brisbane*
  throaty: *Dorchester*
craftwork: *Dalrymple*
cream, antiwrinkle: *Melton
    Constable*
creeps
  gruesome: *Meathop*
  mild: *East Wittering*
crimes, ancient: *Burlingjobb*
crossings
  pedestrian: *Boseman*
  railroad: *Humber*
crotches, trouser: *Botley*
crouches, upward: *Hucknall*
crying: *Babworth*
cubicles
  inaccessible: *Milwaukee*
  horribly soiled: *Wyoming*
cupboards
  jugs in: *Upottery*
  kites in: *Kanturk*
  saucepans in: *Cong*
  skeletons in: *Glemanuilt*
curses, Scottish: *Aird of Sleat*
cushions, by side of the road:
    Edgbaston
customs, charming pointless old:
    Edgbaston

Damocles, the Trewoofe of:
    Trewoofe
dances
  of beer glasses: *Sketty*
  in street: *Droitwich*
darkness, groping for objects in:
    Tegucigalpa
dearies
  lovable mad old: *Bradworthy*
  soporific rabbity old: *Clabby*
decisions, wrong: *Huna*
decorations, Christmas: *Chenies,
    Clovis*
dentists: *Gallipoli, Gipping, Glutt
    Lodge*
  guerrilla: *Beccles*
  violent: *Weem*
deposits, small, black, satisfying:
    Tidpit
desperation
  frankly rushed: *Wyoming*
  polite: *Iping*
desserts, unwanted: *Nutbourne*
determination, bloody-minded:
    Oswestry
devices
  agricultural: *Jarrow*
  humorous: *Barstibley*
dialogue, single page of:
    Clackavoid
diaries, meaningless entries in:
    Epsom
dice: *Hoggeston*
Dickens, Charles: *Smisby*
dirt: *Sutton and Cheam*
disco, people who should have
    been left in the: *Hagnaby*
discrepancies, unaccountable:
    Bodmin
dishwashers: *Dobwalls*
disorder, mental: *Laconia*
dogs
  large, randy, teatime: *Scrabster*

small, moribund: *Scamblesby*
small, repulsive, snuffling:
  Scorrier
small, vicious, yappy: *Baughurst*
dog turds, small but still nasty:
  Bromsgrove
doors
  deliberately obstructive:
    Ramsgate
  revolving, overpopulated:
    Shifnal
  things caused by walking into:
    Sluggan
double glazing, inhabitants of:
  Harbottle
doughnut: *Brymbo*
downstairs bathroom, hats in:
  Tweedsmuir
drawbridges: *Araglin*
drawers, bottom: *Marlow*
dressing tables: *Boolteens*
dribble, infantile: *Halcro*
drink, philosophical state during:
  Solent
drinks, repellent: *Aasleagh, Naas*
drips, gooey, waxen: *Slubbery*
droplets
  hanging, stylish: *Berry Pomeroy*
  mobile: *Longniddry*
  persistent, trouser: *Wimbledon*
drunks
  unappealing: *Pleeley*
  uncomprehending: *Blithbury*
dry, not very: *Wrabness*
duffers
  barking mad old: *Pant-y-Wacco*
  boring old: *Ainderby Quernhow*
  insane sprightly old: *Wivenhoe*
  loathsome merry: *Boothby
    Graffoe*
  pompous old: *Ainderby Steeple*
dwarves, nubile: *Forsinain*

ears
  inner: *Nanhoron*
  outer: *Luffness*
edicts, ancient: *Farduckmanton*
eggs, boiled: *Symond's Yat*
elbows, sore: *Bures*
elevators
  filled with fat people: *Ponka
    City*
  misuse of: *Nybster*
  silence in: *Emsworth*
ends, long, thin, dangling:
  Ranfurly
engineers, telephone: *Lydiard
  Tregoze*
envelopes, dangerous: *Scramoge*
environments, dark, moist:
  Huttoft
epaulettes, useless: *Trossachs*
epiglottis, giant, waggling:
  Ullingswick
erasers, rubber: *Tampa*
escalators, deaf Scandanavian
  tourists who block the: *Ullock*
euphemisms, senseless:
  Fairymount
evenings, wasted: *Lowther*
excrement, airborne: *Burlingjobb*
excuses
  feeble: *Dorridge*
  impromptu but still feeble:
    Hastings
  lame: *Ardscalpsie*
  ludicrous: *Brisbane*
  outrageous: *Ardscull*
  transparent: *Bilbster*
exorcism: *Clenchwarton*
experts, humiliating the: *Aboyne*
expressions
  facial, agonized:
    Minchinhampton
  peculiar: *Banff*
  pissed: *Blithbury*

raging: *Damnaglaur*
sly: *Golant*
vaguely attentive: *Hove*
eyebrows, useless employment of:
  Epping

farts: *see under* noises (if you
  must)
faucets
  embarrassment caused by:
    Botley
  foot-operated: *Polbathic*
  trouser-dousing: *Esher*
feelings
  of fillings: *Tingrith*
  queasy: *Guernsey*
  queasy, bottom-oriented:
    Shoeburyness
  sentimental: *Glasgow*
  uneasy: *Dungeness, Frating
    Green*
feet, elephantine, umbrellas for
  use of: *Clackmannan*
fencing: *Pabbay*
festoonment: *Chipping Ongar*
fifteen years younger, people who
  are: *Glasgow*
fingers, insertion of, into box:
  Cannock Chase
firing: *Tillicoultry*
fish, tropical, stupid: *Stoke Poges*
flaps
  clothy, roomy: *Moffat*
  hairy, sparse: *Scraptoft*
Fleming, Sir Alexander: *Eriboll*
flies: *Harbottle*
floor-matting, indelicate uses of:
  Bures
fluff
  mysterious: *Knaptoft*
  navel: *Lowestoft*
  yellow, motorized: *Memphis*
folds, fleshy: *Lusby*

football players faking:
  Hoddlesden
foreigners
  impersonation of: *Aberbeeg*
  probably deaf or stupid:
    Yarmouth
fowl feeding: *Farduckmanton*
Freemasonry: *Grimsby*
frowning, important: *Frolesworth*
fruit, theft of a single piece of:
  Market Deeping
furniture
  execrable: *Mapledurham*
  lavatorial, frilly: *Ossett*

Gable, Clark: *Epworth*
galoshes: *Burwash, Luffness*
games
  ball: *Hoddlesden, Pelutho*
  board: *Bishop's Caundle,
    Hoggeston*
  indoor: *Aboyne*
  outdoor, East European:
    Twomileborris
gardening
  hopelessness of: *Crail*
  trousers of: *Broats*
gardens, embarrassing talks in:
  Ambleside
garments
  exotic, pretentious: *Shalunt*
  fatuous, foreign: *Valletta*
  gabardine, ankle-length:
    Flodigarry
  peculiar, frightful: *Neen Sollars*
  woolen, knee-length: *Jurby*
gazes, shrewd: *Wroot*
gestures, ambiguous but rude:
  Fovant
gin, price of: *Le Touquet*
girlfriend, long forgotten except
  by wife: *Mavis Enderby*

girls, teenage, in bedroom:
  Tibshelf
gizmos, plastic or metal: *Pimlico*
glances, humorous, at blobs:
  Swanage
glass, pointless tapping on: *Stoke
  Poges*
globules, yellow, gummy,
  unpleasant: *Mugeary*
go, people who just won't: *Clunes*
goats
  jocular tedious old: *Barstibley*
  noisy tuneless old: *Royston*
golfing, overpaid twits who go:
  Kitmurvy
golf strokes, homicidal:
  Whaplode Drove
goo, seagull: *Sutton and Cheam*
good-byes, premature: *Hidcote
  Bartram*
gourmets, slithery: *Berry
  Pomeroy*
grass, intelligent forms of:
  Trispen
gravel, infuriating: *Crail*
Greer, Germaine; *Shrivenham*
guards, railway: *Galashiels*
guilt, powerful: *Glemanuilt*
gurgling, involuntary abdominal:
  Tumby
gusto, terrific, tuneless: *Royston*
gutters, dog's business clogging
  up the: *Dogdyke*

hair
  facial, bizarre; *Scethrog*
  nostril: *Kennewick, Yakima*
  pubic, in moussaka: *Scroggs*
  sprigs of, for chasing ants:
    Monkstoft
hairdressers, mad, Welsh:
  Ardscalpsie

handlebar mustaches, female:
  Lossiemouth
hands, clammy: *Meath*
hangovers, incapacitating:
  Duntish
hankies, worn knotted on head:
  Sidcup
hat behind, leaving one's:
  Hidcote Bartram
hatred, violent, by spouse: *Mavis
  Enderby*
hats
  furry, absurd: *Glinsk*
  gigantic, conical, coolie:
    Valletta
  hanky: *Sidcup*
  large, ill-fitting collection of:
    Tweedsmuir
heads, black: *Quabbs*
hedge, things to do behind one's
  front: *Todber*
hemorrhoid commercials:
  Baraboo
herring fishermen: *Flodigarry*
history, lost in the mists of:
  Hutlerburn
holes
  bath drain: *Polperro*
  things that settle into: *Writtle*
  things that sit on: *Dillytop*
horns
  large, uncomfortable: *Humby*
  long, ceremonial: *Hunsingore*
  moderate-sized but
    unconcealable: *Huby*
  small, Scandinavian:
    Oswaldtwistle
horses, china, rude: *Barstibley*
hotels
  clanking: *Bonkle*
  mock-Tudor: *Melcombe Regis*
hunches, foolish, in the theater:
  Totteridge

hutlers, clumsy: *Hutlerburn*
hymns: *Detchant, Royston*

ice, octogenarians under the:
　Wivenhoe
idea, not having the faintest:
　Epsom, Osbaston
ID cards, left at home: *Margate*
idiots
　ludicrous, deluded:
　　Kibblesworth
　roaring, pretentious: *Haugham*
implements
　curious, horticultural: *Haxby*
　small, stout: *Naseby*
　wooden, silly: *Ibstock*
income tax, impossibility of
　doing: *Swanibost*
incontinence, reptilian: *Dunbar*
indecision, nervous: *Clathy*
infants, small, naked, comical:
　Barstibley
inklings, tiny, stomach-curdling:
　Ely
interesting, someone more than
　you: *Sconser*
intermission, theater bars in the:
　Tabley Superior
into each other, bumping:
　Droitwich
items
　nasal, airborne: *Scronkey*
　prunelike, waterlogged: *Dewlish*
　sticky, clammy: *Belper*
　sticky, furry: *Silloth*
　thin, circular, meaty: *Shanklin*

jackets
　dust: *Liff*
　hairy, stained: *Bradford*
　hideous, casual: *Saffron Walden*
　loud check: *Louth*
　not quite long enough: *Stebbing*

jingles: *Dittisham*
jogging, suicide by means of:
　Kingston Bagpuise
jokes
　mild, for clergymen: *Bude*
　practical: *Araglin*
　practical, spectacular: *Banteer*
　retelling: *Plymouth*

keys, useless bunches of: *Burton
　Coggles*
kilts, hoary old gags about:
　Glenwhilly
kitchen walls: *Smearisary*
knees, sore: *Bures*
knots, intricate: *Kanturk*

laughter, hearty, false: *York*
lawn mowers, frustrated: *Trispen*
leathery flapping bits: *Luppit*
leftovers: *Goosnargh, High Offley*
legs
　extremely unwelcome things up:
　　Scrabster
　things not underneath:
　　Limerigg
　things underneath: *Hucknall*
　unwelcome things down:
　　Wimbledon
　unwelcome things up: *Affpuddle*
　useless: *Clun*
Lewis, Jerry: *Frimley*
licking of envelopes: *Scramoge*
life, the facts of: *Ambleside*
light bulbs, problems of
　disposing of: *Clathy*
limp bread: *Yate*
lines: *Duggleby, Evercreech,
　Foindle, Twomileborris*
literary critics: *Ripon*
loaves, curious-shaped:
　Bradworthy

lobby, great oafs screeching in the: *Haugham*
looks
 lecherous: *Frosses*
 polite, angry: *Evercreech*
 superior, at shoes: *Dubuque*
 superior, in theater: *Tabley Superior*
lounges, cocktail: *Melcombe Regis*
love, unrequited: *Lydiard Tregoze*
lovers, used up by Germaine Greer: *Shrivenham*
luggage, ill-behaved: *Adlestrop*
lumps
 agricultural, aromatic: *Jarrow*
 cardboard, useful: *Ludlow*
 concrete, airborne: *Hodnet*
 disgusting, attached to face: *Kirby*
 dull, in suitcase: *Glassel*
 edible, steaming, unremovable: *Glossop*
 gristly, acrid: *Grimsby*
 gummy, shapeless: *Papcastle*
 insular, inedible: *Hoylake*
 powdery, floating: *Poges*
 rural, underfoot: *Cairnpat*
 small, awkward, dangerous: *Fraddam*
 small, nasal: *Peebles*
 tiny, in swimming trunks: *Lubcroy*
 unwelcome, nocturnal, in front: *Humby*
 unwelcome, nocturnal, underneath: *Tolob*
 unwelcome, urban, all over: *Burlingjobb*
 urban, overhead and underfoot: *Bromsgrove*

mad, you don't have to be, etc.: *Snitterfield*
madmen, departed, in toasters: *Throckmorton*
maneuvers, awkward, leaping: *Hobbs Cross*
manholes, open, amusing: *Frimley*
maps, road: *Kalami, Worgret*
margarine: *Darenth*
mats, small, sopping: *Listowel*
matter, gaseous: *Eriboll*
mattresses
 banana-shaped: *Baumber*
 enormous, muscular: *Harbledown*
maybe, meaning no: *Yesnaby*
measure of luminosity: *Blean*
measures of distance
 parking lots: *Nad*
 sheep: *Sheppey*
 trousers: *Malibu*
measures of time
 art galleries: *Frolesworth*
 camera stores: *Ainsworth*
 elevators: *Emsworth*
meat, ghastly surprises in: *Aigburth*
medallions, gold: *Herstmonceux*
medical science, advances in: *Meeth*
memorials, tops of: *Plympton*
men
 dismal, pedantic, little: *Benburb*
 pathetic, deluded, little: *Brough Sowerby*
 myopic, dangerous, little: *Low Eggborough*
merciless boiling: *Cong*
merry-go-rounds: *Adrigole*
mid-pee, flusing in: *Tincleton*
milk jugs, unnecessary numbers of: *Upottery*

mistakes
  Celtic, computer, spelling:
    Maentwrog
  embarrassing: *Tegucigalpa,*
    Ephrata
  horrifying, unavoidable: *Wigan*
mmm!: *Hoylake*
moats: *Bealings*
modesty, false, female: *Simprim*
moments
  awful: *Umberleigh*
  deeply embarrassing: *Lulworth*
  deeply unexciting: *Emsworth*
  utterly pants-wetting: *Wembley*
monasteries: *Corstorphine*
moods, irrational: *Cranleigh*
moors: *Luffenham, Luffness,*
    Slogarie
morning
  five o'clock in the: *Bonkle*
  two o'clock in the: *Pott Shrigley*
moron, not wanting to be
    thought a: *Frolesworth*
morsels, small, prominent,
    repulsive: *Kirby*
motorcycles
  feeling of new: *Nempnett*
    Thrubwell
  involuntary impersonation of:
    Berepper
moussaka, stout pubes in:
    Scroggs
movements
  bowel: *Glororum*
  fishlike: *Gipping*
  flabby: *Humber*
  futile, at home: *Kelling*
  futile, at post offices: *Stoke*
    Poges
  futile, at waiters: *Epping*
  vague, manual, searching:
    Scosthrop
  waggling, artistic: *Llanelli*

movies, just three minutes from:
    Yonder Bognie
mumbling, as a career:
    Woolfardisworthy
Murmansk, things that shouldn't
    be in: *Glentaggart*
mush, dehydrated: *Pott Shrigley*

'n': *Nacton*
names, forgetting of: *Golant*
nastiness, hard-boiled: *Dobwalls*
Neapolitan tubs, fist shoved into:
    Blean
nerds
  incredible little: *Corfu*
  lanky, Scandinavian: *Ullock*
  piddling, in your toilet:
    Tincleton
New York
  cabby: *Lackawanna*
  crazy: *Zebulon*
  potholes: *Warwarsing*
news, astounding: *Jawcraig*
newspaper clippings, comical:
    Snitter
newspapers, fascination of other
    people's: *Corfe*
nipples, high-profile: *Budby*
nitwits, great steaming: *Duggleby*
no, expressed as yes: *Yesnaby*
nodules, rubber: *Pimperne*
nods, surly, from behind hedge:
    Todber
noises
  bubbling and inopportune:
    Tumby
  burbling and nocturnal: *Bonkle*
  discreet but unwelcome: *Affcot*
  distant and meaningless:
    Amersham
  grunting and considerate:
    Horton-cum-Studley
  grunting and satisfied: *Poona*

gurgling and milky: *Pitlochry*
gushing and cooing: *Oshkosh*
humming and whistling:
 Burleston
humming, whistling, and
 chanting: *Milwaukee*
loud and clattering:
 Clackmannan
loud and embarrassing:
 Berepper
loud and informative: *Taroom*
loud and rattling: *Hoggeston*
mumbling, uninterested:
 Nazeing
painful and squeaky:
 Skibbereen
quiet and rubbery: *Tampa*
screeching, Celtic: *Lochranza*
screeching, infantile:
 Caarnduncan
screeching, rural: *Mellon
 Udrigle*
squeaky, nylonish: *Screeb*
tatatting and satisfying: *Ibstock*
ticketatacketaticketing: *Seattle*
ticketatacktackatuckaticketing:
 Trantlemore
tiny and embarrassing:
 Brompton
tooting and puzzling:
 Whissendine
trumpeting, hippopotamoid:
 Brompton
whiffling, in elevators: *Burbage*
whirring and chuntering:
 Ipswich
noses
 bleeding: *Burton Coggles*
 erstwhile contents of:
 Longniddry, Snohomish
 excreta, malleable: *Skegness*
 exterior features of: *Botolphs*
 fascinating items in:

 Massachussets
 noises made with: *Burbage*
 things that come down from:
 Des Moines
 tools for stuffing into:
 Botusfleming
nostalgic yearnings: *Aberystwyth*
nozzles, aircraft, strange powers
 over: *Ventnor*
number, wrong, so she claims:
 Kurdistan

objects
 banana-shaped: *Baumber*
 clammy, inedible: *Amlwch*
 deformed: *Duddo*
 elephantine: *Clackmannan*
 fantastically dull: *Lamlash*
 frilly: *Ossett*
 gross: *Cairnpat*
 heavy, with toes on: *Clun*
 horrible, roomy: *Mapledurham*
 long-handled: *Botusfleming*
 lost, found again: *Winkley*
 plastic, pretentious: *Brumby*
 small, boring: *Nazeing*
 small, priceless, in pieces: *Tyne
 and Wear*
 sticky, permanent: *Dipple*
 sticky, wooden: *Cotterstock*
 strange, culinary: *Cong*
 tiny, disgusting: *Chipping
 Ongar*
 tiny, pointless: *Didcot*
 unappealing, lonely: *Brymbo*
 wet, cold, enormous: *Trewoofe*
 with bumps on: *Bolsover*
 with holes in, artistic:
 Bromsgrove, Dalrymple
officers, retired, army, raving:
 Panty-y-Wacco
offices, inhabitants of: *Brough
 Sowerby, Clovis, Snitterby*

office walls, comical clippings on: *Snitter*
Olsson, Nigel: *Throcking*
ooze, yellow: *Clonmult*
orchestra pits, spittle in: *Ullapool*
orchestras, people who conduct from audience: *Thrumster*
orgasm, multiple: *Papworth Everard*
ornaments, misapplied: *Bishop's Caundle*
overalls, inky: *Hibbing*

pain
  rising above: *Wike*
  sudden: *Acle*
  tools for inflicting: *Weem*
pain and shame: *Yonkers*
paintbrushes, cheap: *Aith*
paint smudges, expensive: *Dalrymple*
paint stirrers: *Cotterstock*
pajamas, Muslim: *Albuquerque*
pangs, terrible: *Lydiard Tregoze*
panic
  in airport: *Hever*
  in bathroom: *Great Wakering*
  in corridor: *Ditherington*
panther sweat, erotic properties of: *Dunbar*
parkas, nylon: *Screeb*
parked cars, honking at: *Tooting Bec*
parking lots, automatic: *Nad*
particles, nasal: *Massachussets*
parties
  anger after: *Heanton Punchardon*
  crud under sofa after: *Silloth*
  dreadful guests at: *Nubbock, Oughterby*
  drink running out at: *Aasleagh*
  Hollywood: *Snohomish*

jerks you can't get away from at: *East Wittering*
  teenage, steamy: *Frosses*
parts, private, had by dog for lunch: *Scorrier*
parts of speech, crucial, obscured: *Dorchester*
patches, wet, underarm: *Pitsligo*
patches, wet, under-bottom: *Hobbs Cross*
paving stones: *Affpuddle*
pebbles, wet, shiny: *Glassel*
pee, inability to with audience present: *Kettleness*
peer groups: *Caarnduncan*
pellets, unmentionable: *Peebles*
pencil sharpenings, giant: *Blitterlees*
penises, moist: *Wetwang*
pens, lack of: *Aynho*
people
  cringing, irritating: *Greeley*
  frantic, disorganized: *Worksop*
  large groups of helpful grunting: *Horton-cum-Studley*
  large groups of miserly: *Bodmin*
  medium-sized clumps of enraged: *Dolgellau*
  niggling: *Scranton*
  small families of horrible: *Molesby*
  smooth, greedy: *Winston-Salem*
  underprivileged, leg-wise: *Wigan*
  unshaven, maddening: *Draffan*
  vast, wobble-cheeked: *Humber*
  who give themselves the biggest slice: *Finuge*
perpetuity, in: *Cotterstock*
photographs, passport: *Banff*
picnic spots
  mildly uncomfortable: *Munderfield*
  splattered with gore: *Meathop*

pig-out: *Berkhamsted*
pigs, matching: *Tibshelf*
piles, unstable: *Boscastle*
pillows: *Abilene*
pimples, volcanic: *Bilbster*
pins
  danger: *Acle*
  safety: *Lubcroy*
pipers: *Lochranza*
places, safe: *Fiunary*
plastic wrap: *Amlwch*
pleasure, idiosyncratic, revolting:
  Glororum
plucking of nostril hairs: *Yonkers*
plugs, bath: *Dillytop,
  Twomileborris*
plumbing noises: *Bonkle*
pockets
  omnivorous: *Nantucket*
  upholstered: *Hassop*
points, sound made by trains
  crossing: *Trantlemore*
poles, strong desire to grasp:
  Abercrave
police: *Tolstachaolais*
policemen, skin of: *Melton
  Constable*
politicians
  rabid, left-wing, rich: *Quedgeley*
  ridiculous, furry-hatted: *Glinsk*
polo: *Ganges*
poltergeists, resident in car:
  Worgret
poodles, glass: *Tibshelf*
pools, warm, edible: *Hoylake*
pornography, the making of:
  Papworth Everard
positions, switches that seem to
  be off in both: *Ockle*
potatoes
  fear of: *Peoria*
  misshapen: *Duddo*

pouches, small, humorous:
  Glenwhilly
poultry keepers: *Goosecruives*
prefaces: *Querrin*
prongs
  clogged with sludge: *Henstridge*
  concealed: *Hadzor*
  truncated: *Baldock*
prunelike extremities: *Dewlish*
puddles
  exterior: *Affpuddle, Burwash*
  interior: *Goole, Sketty*
punishment, capital, in schools:
  Little Urswick
purpose, unfathomable: *Haxby*
pus, scarlet: *Buldoo*
pyramids, metallic: *Boscastle*

races, three-legged: *Shifnal*
raincoats, expensive: *Trossachs*
rashes, leg: *Ganges*
rattling, senseless: *Amersham*
reactions, chemical, unedifying:
  Bradford
refrigerators
  congealed matter in: *Goosnargh*
  cleaning out unexpectedly:
    Cushing
  damp things in: *Nantwich*
  teeming with life: *Guernsey*
remarks, own, rather amusing,
  unheard: *Dorchester,
  Umberleigh*
requests, whining, unwelcome:
  Quall
restaurants
  unfussy, unusual menu: *Curry
  Mallet*
  polite maître d': *Elmira*
revelations, personal, with
  stomach rumble: *Tumby*
Richard III: Oundle

rights, ancient, with midgets: *Forsinain*
rock
  loud and boring: *Throcking*
  loud and persistent: *Dittisham*
  quiet and persistent: *Crail*
rubbish, vital: *Nottage*
rugs, horseshoe-shaped, fluffy: *Luton*
rulers, noises made by: *Thrupp*
runs, token: *Sturry*
Russian hater: *Blount*

safe places: *Fiunary*
salami: *Shanklin*
sandwiches
  bacon: *Beccles*
  clean: *Amlwch*
  in London: *Darenth*
sarong, appearing in lobby wearing a: *Valletta*
saunters, carefree: *Frimley*
sausages: *Kerry*
scabs, amorous: *Bures*
schoolteachers: *Bradford*
scissors, looking for: *Scosthrop*
scribbles: *Screggan*
seats
  aircraft: *Rochester*
  toilet: *Luton*
secretions, in hamburger joints: *Clonmult*
secrets, sharing: *Marytavy*
self-knowledge, serene, completely wrong: *Solent*
sensations, lurching: *Bedfont*
sentences, finishing other people's: *Happle*
services
  church: *Detchant, Royston*
  monastic: *Corstorphine*

seven miles of concealed moorland: *Slogarie*
Severinsen, Doc: *Saffron Walden*
sex, lurid, imaginary: *Sligo*
shades of green
  domestic: *Gretna Green*
  institutional: *Frating Green*
shapes, rude, confusable: *Tegucigalpa*
shaving: *Hathersage*
sheds
  nuclear: *Low Eggborough*
  potting: *Haxby*
  tool: *Cotterstock*
sheep
  mysterious complaints of: *Jawcraig*
  woolly charm of in distance: *Sheppey*
shifting, anxious: *Iping*
shirts
  beer down: *Tulsa*
  open to waist: *Herstmonceux*
  stabbing: *Acle*
shoes, wrong sort of: *Dubuque*
shops, dress: *Dolgellau*
shouting at foreigners: *Yarmouth*
showers, agonizing: *Alltami*
sick, off wrong side of boat: *Silesia*
side
  things on the other: *Quenby*
  things that stick out the: *Aith*
  things written on the: *Dorridge*
sideburns, extensive, scrofulous: *Galashiels*
silences, ghastly: *Lulworth*
singers, carol, hiding from: *Fulking*
sixteen-year-olds in heat: *Frosses*
six times before, stories heard: *Smarden*
skiing: *Zeal Monachorum*

skin
 flaps of: *Scopwick*
 twists of: *Kerry*
sleep
 muck in eyes after: *Mugeary*
 things that shouldn't have gone
  to: *Clun*
sludge, brittle: *Cromarty*
smells, horrible: *Keele*
smiles
 frozen, horrified: *Sneem*
 grim, determined: *Smarden*
 shiny, meaningless: *Ewelme*
smoking, excuses for: *Brisbane*
smutty postcards: *Snitterfield*
snacks, nasty: *Nantwich*
sneeze, failure to: *Amersham*
snippets, hairy: *Hathersage*
snow, wedges of lurking:
  Trewoofe
socks, contents of: *Skenfrith*
sofa, things spotted from:
  Chenies
something or other, profound
  feelings of: *Hambledon*
sopping, shopping: *Sotterley*
soup
 exotic, made from moats:
  Bealings
 instant: *Poges*
 spattered: *Papple*
 tomato: *Scranton*
space and timelessness:
  Hambledon
spasms, massive facial: *Jawcraig*
spit: *Gallipoli*
spoonful, eggy: *Symond's Yat*
sprigs, dangling, colorful:
  Chenies
squeezing
 cosmetic: *Quabbs*
 religious: *Clenchwarton*
squiggles, financial: *Albuquerque*

stains
 inky: *Hibbing*
 trousers, not own fault: *Botley*
 trousers, own fault:
  Piddletrenthide
staircases, winding: *Harbledown*
stairs
 disappearing: *High Limerigg,
  Limerigg*
 falling down the: *Blean*
standing, ways of: *Ahenny*
standing about: *Lowther*
standing and wondering: *Woking*
stares, harsh, meaningful:
  Kurdistan
stars, film: *Sligo*
Star Trek: *Clackavoid*
steps, small, irrevocable: *Glenties*
stew, ghastly items found in:
  Grimsby
Stewart, Rod: *Dittisham*
sticks, walking: *Clackmannan*
stockings, nylon: *Brecon*
stores
 camera, maddening: *Ainsworth*
 shoe: *Kibblesworth*
 with stupid names: *Drebley*
stories
 endless, repetitive, celebrity:
  Boothby Graffoe
 humorous, interminable:
  Gildersome
strange powers over aircraft
  nozzles: *Ventnor*
streets, cleaning of: *Vancouver*
strips, grimy: *Torlundy*
stubble
 in basin: *Hathersage*
 in sandwiches: *Munderfield*
stumps, tree: *Baldock*
substances
 gray, gummy: *Deal*
 gray, squashy: *Skegness*

120

green, synthetic: *Halifax*
ocher, indelicate: *Quabbs*
various colors, gushing: *Toronto*
white, flaky: *Skenfrith*
yellow, dried: *Henstridge*
yellow, squelchy: *Mugeary*
sunbathing: *Kettering,*
Kimmeridge
suspicions
  horrible: *Mankinholes*
  of infidelity: *Kurdistan*
swigs, nasty surprises in:
Slumbay
switches, useless: *Ockle*

table, refusal to help setting the:
Nanhoron
tables
  antique, priceless, ruined:
Glossop
  dressing cluttered with garbage:
Boolteens, Lamlash
  wobbly: *Ludlow*
tactics
  diversionary: *Swanage*
  thwarted: *Aboyne*
talking, unlikelihood of stopping:
Hove
tampons, politely offering
  around: *Tegucigalpa*
tarpaulins: *Flodigarry*
taxi drivers: *Fovant*
taxis
  seductive remarks in: *Low*
Ardwell
  smell of: *Duluth*
teaspoon, the ultimate: *Scullet*
teeth, smiling determinedly
  through: *Smarden*
telephone directories, collectors
  of antique: *Aldclune*
telephones: *Harpenden,*
Kurdistan, Clebit

terrain, mountainous, with hiker
  spoor: *Cairnpat*
theater, practices in: *Hickling,*
Tabley Superior, Totteridge
things
  moving: *Hesperia*
  spray, for ironing:
Perranzabuloe
  various: *Sutton and Cheam*
three-card monte, winners at:
Tigharry
ties: *Ranfurly*
tips, felt: *Scremby*
toast: *Burnt Yates*
toasters: *Throckmorton, Yate*
toenails, contents of: *Tidpit*
toes, slime on: *Deal*
tongs, silver, for poking
  Freemasons: *Grimsby*
tools, painful, oral: *Weem*
towels, damp: *Wrabness*
tractors, dung-spreading: *Jarrow*
trains
  impersonation of: *Seattle,*
Trantlemore
  royal: *Didcot*
  departed without one:
Dunboyne
  tickets: *Nantucket*
tramps, mad, jabbering:
Theakstone
travel, evidence of: *Tuamgraney*
tripping over carpet: *Thurnby*
trolleys, rogue: *Motspur*
trousers
  elderly: *Broats*
  inflatable: *Huby*
  roguish: *Minchinhampton*
  soaking: *Esher*
  stained: *Botley, Piddletrenthide*
  too long: *Malibu*
  wooden: *Goosecruives*
  wrong pair of: *Duggleby*

trucks, street-cleaning: *Vancouver*
trunks, swimming: *Lubcroy*
truth, palpable: *Hoff*
twerps, bicycle-oriented: *Wormelow Tump*
twitching, uncontrollable: *West Wittering*
twits, annoying: *Thrumster*

umbrella stands: *Clackmannan*
underblankets, lumpy: *Tolob*
underclothes, bestrewn: *Adlestrop*
underpants, half of: *Scrabby*
undressing, watching other people: *Beaulieu Hill*
urges, violent: *Kent*
ushers: *Blean*

vagueness, brisk: *Clixby*
vampire attacks: *Spittal of Glenshee*
veneer, chipboard: *Mapledurham*
virgins, absence of at weddings: *Shirmers*

wads, misshapen, squashy: *Pudsey*
waggling, theatrical: *Llanelli*
waiters
  blind: *Epping*
  dozy: *Aynho*
walks, silly: *Goadby Marwood*
wallets: *Whasset*
walls
  daubed: *Smearisary*
  satisfying: *Skellow*

wartlike objects: *Kirby Misperton*
washing
  failure to finish properly: *Abinger*
  nasty things in the: *Hadzor*
waves
  token: *Sturry*
  unnecessary: *Largoward*
  up trousers: *Malibu*
way up, teeth put back the wrong: *Gipping*
weddings, smoothies at: *Shirmers*
wee-wee, humorous, artificial: *Barstibley*
Welsh hairdressers: *Ardscalpsie, Ardscull*
Welsh rabbit, growths on: *Eriboll*
whodunits: *Didling*
willies, insufficiently waggled: *Piddletrenthide*
Wind, Gone With the: Epworth
Windbreakers: *Savernake*
wing, left: *Quedgeley*
wiped out: *Swanibost*
wipers, windshield: *Memphis*
women, cleaning: *Clabby*
Woolf, Virginia: *York*
words, hatefulness of certain: *Quoyness*
wounds
  on elbows: *Bures*
  during haircut: *Ardscull*
wrong
  gone terribly: *Ely*
  place, heart in the: *Willimantic*

yes, meaning no: *Yesnaby*

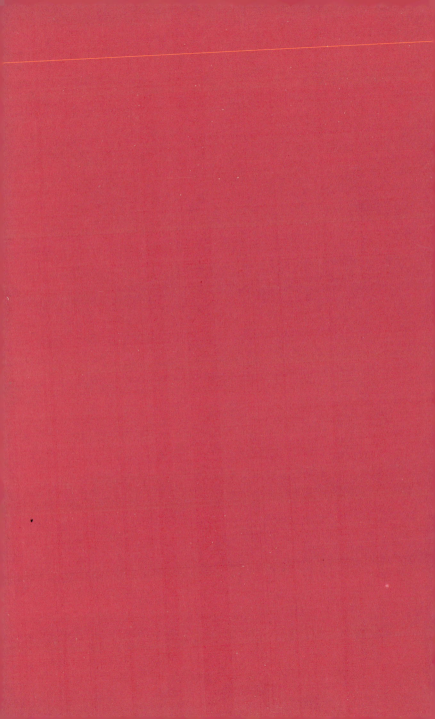